Royal Cavalcade

MARYLIAN WATNEY

Royal Cavalcade

A HISTORY OF THE CARRIAGES AND
TRANSPORT OF ENGLISH KINGS AND QUEENS,
FROM ELIZABETH I ONWARDS

J.A. ALLEN   LONDON

First published in Great Britain by
J.A. Allen & Co Ltd
1 Lower Grosvenor Place
Buckingham Palace Road
London SW1W OEL
1987

British Library Cataloguing in Publication Data

Watney, Marylian
Royal cavalcade: a history of the
carriages and transport of English
kings and queens from Elizabeth I
onwards
1. Carriages and carts—Great
Britain—History 2. Great Britain
—Kings and rulers
I. Title
686.6   TS2025

ISBN 0-85131-440-6

Typeset and Printed by BAS Printers Limited,
Over Wallop, Hampshire

Contents

Acknowledgements 6

Foreword by Lt. Colonel Sir John Miller, GCVO, DSO, MC 7

Introduction *8*

Queen Elizabeth I *11*

King James I *14*

King Charles I *15*

Oliver Cromwell *16*

King Charles II *17*

King James II *19*

William and Mary *19*

Queen Anne *20*

King George I *21*

King George II *22*

King George III *23*

King George IV *28*

King William IV *37*

Queen Victoria *39*

King Edward VII *55*

King George V *66*

King George VI *75*

Queen Elizabeth II *80*

Bibliography *94*

Index *95*

✑ Acknowledgements ✑

THE PUBLISHERS and I are deeply grateful to Her Majesty The Queen for having graciously granted permission for the publication of this book, and for the reproduction of paintings and photographs from the Royal Collection, as well as material from the Royal Archives. We are also indebted to Sir John Miller, the Crown Equerry, for his help and encouragement; to Sir Oliver Millar, Surveyor of The Queen's pictures and Mrs Amanda Dickson; to Mr Oliver Everett, the Royal Librarian; to Miss Elizabeth Cuthbert, Registrar; and Miss Frances Dimond, Curator to the Royal Archives.

I would also like to record my gratitude to the many authors of books listed in the Bibliography, each one of which has provided insights on Royalty and their interest in horses and carriages.

Of great help too were the following: Mrs J. Appelbee, who supplied photographs taken by the late Mr John Scott; Mr G. Eames, AMPA; Mr D.W. Fuller, of Arthur Ackermann & Sons, for photographs of pictures and prints; Mr Douglas Keay, for a photograph from his biography of Queen Elizabeth, the Queen Mother; the late Mr Harold Nockolds, former Archivist to the Worshipful Company of Coachmakers and Coach Harnessmakers; Mr N.C. Selway, for photographs of paintings from his book *The Golden Age of Coaching & Sport*; Mr R. Strang, MRCVS, for the loan of a book which belonged to his grandfather, containing photographs of Royal carriages on view at the 1851 Great Exhibition; to Aberdeen Journals Ltd; Alpha Photographic Press Agency Ltd; British Museum; Central Press Photos Ltd; Mr Findlay Davidson; *Illustrated London News*; Keystone Press Agency; Photo News Agency; Planet News Ltd; Radio Times Hulton Picture Library; Royal Academy of Arts; Royal College of Arms; Sir Geoffrey Shakerley, Bart; Sport & General Agency; *Sunday Telegraph Magazine*; Tate Gallery; *The Times*; and His Grace the Duke of Westminster, DL.

Since the therapy of pony driving for the disabled was originally thought of by HRH The Duke of Edinburgh, it seems appropriate that all proceeds from the sale of this book should go to the Sanders Watney Trust – the fund for disabled driving set up by the British Driving Society as a memorial to my late husband, who was its Founder President. I therefore hope that not only will the book do well, but that readers will enjoy it as much as I did during its research and production.

MARYLIAN WATNEY
JUNE, 1987

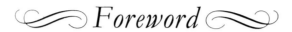

Foreword

By Lieutenant Colonel Sir John Miller, GCVO, DSO, MC

MRS WATNEY has done an immense amount of research to compile *Royal Cavalcade*, and there can be nobody more qualified than her to do this, because the combined experience of herself and her late husband Sandy Watney on all matters appertaining to carriages, harness and driving horses must be unsurpassed.

For historians, *Royal Cavalcade* is important and for those with a particular interest in horse transport it will have special appeal. It is attractively produced and above all it is a most complete and accurate record of Royal travel through the long era of the horse as a means of transport, and brings travel by carriage right into twentieth-century ceremonial and into carriage driving as an exciting and rapidly expanding sport.

I congratulate Mrs Watney and commend this book to a wide circle of readers, and hope that its proceeds will benefit Driving for the Disabled which is so very worthwhile.

John Miller.

~~Introduction~~

TRANSPORT and its development makes fascinating history, and the invention of the wheel made as great an impact upon civilisation as the internal combustion engine was to do in later years. The Egyptians are believed to have been the originators of wheels, the first vehicles probably having been the waggons and chariots mentioned in the Old Testament.

It was not, however, until about 1360 that 'charettes' are spoken of in England, and it is thought that this word can be traced back to the Roman 'currus', 'car', and 'charette' – which was eventually to become 'chariot'. It is surprising, therefore, that in England, horse-drawn carriages do not appear to have been built for Royalty until the reigns of Queen Mary Tudor, and her half-sister Queen Elizabeth I. Previously, litters fixed onto two poles were strapped between a couple of horses in tandem, or else carried on the shoulders of four or more men, and there are illustrations of Queen Elizabeth I being transported in this manner, and by both these means.

Proof that carriage-building then developed lies in the granting of a Charter in 1677 to the Worshipful Company of Coachmakers and Coach Harnessmakers in the City of London. Sadly, however, very few monarchs appear to have been depicted travelling in their carriages, but perhaps this was because English kings preferred to be portrayed riding on horseback.

Today, the earliest Royal carriage in existence is the *'very superb'* Gold State Coach built in 1762 for His Majesty King George III, which has miraculously survived two world wars and has been used for coronations ever since King William IV came to the throne in 1830.

It was during the reign of King George IV, however, that carriages began to be built on lighter and more elegant lines. This was partly due to the great improvements in road surfaces achieved by the engineers, Telford and Macadam, but mostly on account of His Majesty's interest in driving when he was Prince of Wales. But, sadly, although there are several paintings and drawings of the various types of carriage which he drove, none of the actual vehicles has survived.

Queen Victoria's reign was the one in which carriage-building really reached its peak, and particularly at the time of the Great Exhibition held in Hyde Park in 1851, when British coachbuilding received the accolade of being described as '*the envy of the world*'.

Throughout these centuries members of the Royal Family frequently drove themselves about in small vehicles such as phaetons (pronounced 'faytons'), chaises, dog-carts, and gigs, drawn by either one or two ponies, or horses. Some of these are on view at the Royal Mews, but it is the larger, more impressive-looking carriages used on State occasions which capture the imagination and are of the most interest to the general public.

Of these, second in importance to King George III's Gold State Coach, is the Irish State Coach (built in Dublin) which is used by The Queen for the State Opening of Parliament among other functions (its counterpart in Scotland is the Scottish State Coach). Third comes the massive State Landau, which was originally built for King Edward VII and was used by Prince Charles for his wedding in 1981.

Next are: Queen Alexandra's State Coach; the Glass Coach; and the Town Coach. Perhaps it should be explained here that the word 'coach' signifies a vehicle which is *permanently* enclosed by having a solid roof and upper side-panels, the latter now usually fitted with glass.

Also on show are several State and Semi-State Landaus (pronounced 'landors'), the distinction between them being the quantity of decoration and cyphers painted on their panels. These seat four people and have two folding leather hoods which can be raised to join each other so that, in wet weather, the occupants can be completely enclosed, as in a coach. These are followed by Barouches (pronounced 'barooshes'), which have forward-facing seats for only two passengers, with a single folding leather hood to cover them. Barouches are the carriages most resembling babies' perambulators, and in the old days these latter were painted to match their larger counterparts.

All these vehicles can be driven either by postillions, who ride the near-side horses, or by a coachman sitting on a box-seat covered by an ornate tasselled 'hammer-cloth'. Here another explanation may be of interest, for the name 'hammer-cloth' has been a source of much speculation. Some have suggested that it covered a box containing a hammer (among other tools); others that it was derived from 'hammock', since the seat beneath it is of that shape; but the most logical derivation is that under the seat is a space in which a large leather container can be fitted, and in this, hampers of food were frequently stored when long journeys were undertaken. This latter explanation appears in a printed *Servant's Guide and Directory* for the year 1830.

Altogether smaller, enclosed vehicles for two passengers, driven only from the box, and with either a single or else a pair of horses, are the Broughams (pronounced 'broo-ems'), which were previously used by members of the Royal Household. In her book, *Thatched with Gold*, Mabell Countess of Airlie tells of the nice distinction drawn during the reign of King George V, when *Ladies* of Queen Mary's Bedchamber were allowed the use of two horses, while *Women* of the Bedchamber were permitted only one!

Introduction

Broughams were made very popular by Lord Brougham during Queen Victoria's reign and they, and their larger counterparts, Clarences, were found to be so convenient for driving about town that when discarded by their owners, they were converted into street cabs. On account of the noise they made in transit, they were nicknamed 'Growlers'.

Throughout this text the words 'carriage' and 'vehicle' have been used as general terms for any type of horse-drawn conveyance. The word 'carriage', however, originally referred to what is now known as an *under*-carriage and, according to Mr William Felton, whose treatise on coachbuilding was published in 1794, a carriage was that part of a vehicle which *'bears the stress of the whole machine, and much depends on its sufficiency'*. However, even Mr Felton himself admitted that this word also implied *'a carriage complete'*, and this appears to have remained the case ever since.

Within the Royal Mews other exhibits include sleighs, harness, saddlery and liveries, as well as numerous pictures, photographs, and other items of memorabilia. Similar, though smaller, exhibitions are open to the public at both Windsor Castle and Hampton Court. All have contributed to the staging of many Royal cavalcades.

Queen Elizabeth I

ALTHOUGH Queen Mary I is said to have been driven to her coronation in 1553 in a chariot drawn by six horses, no further details appear to have been recorded. It seems curious, therefore, that five years later, when her half-sister, Queen Elizabeth I, came to the throne, no vehicle appears to have been available, and she attended her coronation in 1559 in a litter slung between two horses in tandem. Unimpressive as this may sound, Queen Elizabeth's coronation procession was in fact very spectacular, as is revealed in an illustrated book which recorded everyone who took part and which is still in existence in the archives of the Royal College of Heralds.

One year later, however, the Queen is recorded as having received her first vehicle: a massive coach, made in Holland; while in 1564, William Boonen, its reported donor, is believed to have become her coachman. The Queen's first State Coach, also a large vehicle and open at the sides so that she was visible to the public, was built by Walter Rippon and was first used in 1571 for the State Opening of Parliament.

It was not until she had reigned for twenty-six years that anything more is known about the Queen's carriages, which, by this time, had increased in number. These were reported on by Lupold von Wedel, a Pomeranian nobleman who visited England in 1584, and his descriptions make fascinating reading since many tally with engravings still in existence.

For example, after attending a dinner at Hampton Court, he wrote:

> '*We saw The Queen's horses, eighty-one in number, and three carriages. One was very small, only two persons being able to sit in it. The distance between the fore and hind wheels was very large. The second carriage was lined with red leather, fastened with silver-gilt nails; and on the third carriage, the wheels, being twelve in number, were fixed under the axle in a manner very difficult to describe.*'

He related further that on November 12th the Queen made her entrance into London '*to a house near the beginning of the town, called St James's, where, in former times, the young English Kings used to be brought up*' and that:

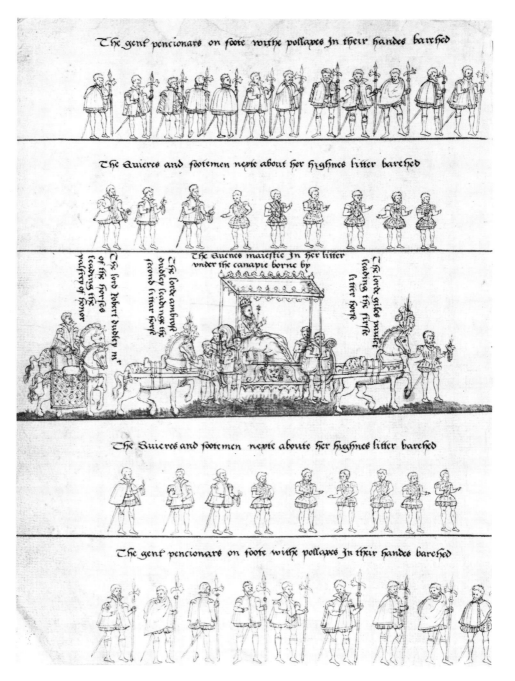

The gent pencionars on foote withe pollaxes in their handes barehed

The Quieres and footemen nere about her highnes litter barehed

The Quenes maiestie in her litter under the canapie borne by

The lord Robert dudley mr of the horses leading the palfrey of honor

The lorde ambrose dudley leading the second litter horse

The lorde giles pawlet leading the firste litter horse

The Quieres and footemen nere aboute her highnes litter barehed

The gent pencionars on foote withe pollaxes in their handes barehed

A page from the book produced by the Royal College of Arms which depicted the processional order at the coronation of Queen Elizabeth I in 1559. This shows that Her Majesty was conveyed in a litter slung between two horses, one behind the other. (Photo courtesy of Royal College of Arms)

Detail from a print in the British Museum which shows Queen Elizabeth I in her coach in 1582, two years before the visit recorded by the Pomeranian nobleman, whose description of one of her coaches tallies with this drawing. (Photo: British Museum)

'The Queen sat in an open gilt carriage, under a canopy of red velvet embroidered with gold and pearls. In the front and back parts of the carriage were fastened three plumes of various colours,* and four brown horses, royally attired, were harnessed to the carriage. She sat alone in the carriage, being clad in a white robe ... and looked like goddesses are wont to be painted. Behind the Queen's carriage rode Milord Leicester, a count of princely rank, who acted a long time as Master of the Horse. ... After came a gilt carriage embroidered with gold and silver, but not equal to the Queen's carriage, and another vehicle of leather ornamented with yellow nails, both were empty.'

On a later date in November he recorded yet another Royal appearance:

'Now followed The Queen in a half-covered Sedan chair, which looked like a half-covered bed. The chair and cushions on which The Queen was seated were covered with gold

---

*The use of coloured feathers as decorations on carriages does not appear to have persisted, but *black* plumes on both hearses and horses' heads were used in funeral processions until horse-drawn transport came to an end in the early 1900s.

and silver cloth; the Sedan chair was carried by two cream-coloured horses with yellow manes and tails; and after which came two empty carriages, the one lined with red, the other with black velvet embroidered with gold.'

Mention of cream-coloured horses is unusual at this time since they are reported as not having been introduced into England until the reign of George I, but these may have been two of the six Hungarian greys purchased from Holland in 1581, which had their manes and tails dyed a tawny shade of orange. It is also interesting to hear that Queen Elizabeth had reverted to being transported in a litter – perhaps this was a re-staging of her original coronation procession.

Throughout her forty-five years on the throne, Queen Elizabeth made many journeys throughout the country, and travelled frequently between St James's Palace and Hampton Court, as well as to the Palace at Richmond in Surrey. When visiting the latter, however, she used to cross the River Thames to Mortlake, where she often called upon her Court Astrologer, Dr John Dee. (A glance at the map will show why Mortlake was an important landing stage, for the twisting course of the Thames is such that even today in a motorboat, the journey from there to Richmond takes about an hour, whereas by road it is not more than fifteen or twenty minutes.)

The last of her journeys here was made in 1603, for on the 24th day of March that year, Queen Elizabeth I – England's 'Good Queen Bess' – died at the Palace of Richmond, and with her the Tudor dynasty.

⮞ *King James I* ⮜

UPON hearing of the death of Queen Elizabeth, King James I, who, as the son of Mary, Queen of Scots, had already been proclaimed James VI of Scotland, decided to leave immediately for England, and although carriages were available, he is quoted as having said: '*I will have no coach, for the people are desirous to see a King, and so they shall as well see his body as his face,*' and though it was said that he was not a good rider, he mounted a horse and set out for the South.

It was during his reign that glass was first produced, but, fearing that a shortage of trees might result, the King forbade its manufacture if wood was to be used as fuel. Within twenty-five years, however, coal was being used, and so glass windows began to be fitted into the side-panels of coaches.

✑ King Charles I ✑

BY 1625, when King Charles I came to the throne, more carriages were in circulation. So much so that in 1634 Sir Sanders Duncomb was granted a licence for the letting out of sedan chairs as it was said that: *'the streetes of Westminster are of late so much encumbered and pestered with the unnecessary multitude of coaches therein used.'* By the following year, however, the congestion was such that the King issued a proclamation that: *'the general and promiscuous use'* of hackney coaches was causing *'disturbance to the King and Queen personally; pesters the streetes; breaks up the pavements, and causes increase in the price of forage.'* For this reason coaches were forbidden in London *'except to travel three miles out of same.'*

This proclamation apparently had the desired effect, for by 1637 there were said to have been no more than sixty hackney carriages in London. The King, however, could not have been worried by the possibility of further congestion, for in 1641 he was granting licences for the importing of coach-horses, specifying that they should be *'not under 14 hands high.'*

A drawing of a coach built at the time of, and most probably for, King Charles I. (From A History of Coaches *by G.A. Thrupp)*

Oliver Cromwell

ALTHOUGH Oliver Cromwell was not of Royal blood, he took over the running of the country after the execution of Charles I in 1649, eventually becoming the 'Lord Protector of England' with the title 'His Highness'. But in addition to his political and military achievements, he has also gone down in history as having had an accident while driving in Hyde Park!

This occurred in 1654 when Cromwell, who was described as *'not being one who excels in driving a chariot to the goal'*, decided to take the reins from his coachman and drive himself. This, according to the Dutch Ambassador, proved the potential danger of the fashion for harnessing teams of horses with only the leading pair being driven by a postillion rider. The Dutch Ambassador wrote that Cromwell:

> *'drove pretty handsomely for some time. But at last provoking the horses too much with the whip, they grew unruly and ran so fast that the postillion could not hold them in, whereby His Highness was flung out of the coach box upon the pole.'*

Another, similar, account of this accident was provided by a Colonel Ludlow, who said that after Cromwell had been thrown out *'his pistol fired in his pocket, though without hurt to himself'* and added *'by which means he might have been instructed how dangerous it was to meddle with those things wherein he had no experience.'*

Interestingly, both writers describe the horses as the 'six greys' presented to Cromwell by the Count (or Duke) or Oldenburg; the German breed of Oldenburgs are still extremely popular as coach-horses and some are in the Royal Mews today.

Opposite: King Charles II leaving Hampton Court in a coach drawn by six black horses. As can be seen, the coach is more enclosed than those used by Queen Elizabeth I, and feathers no longer appear on the roof. (Reproduced by gracious permission of Her Majesty The Queen)

~ *King Charles II* ~

THE REIGN OF King Charles II – which began in 1660, after Cromwell's son and heir, Richard, had fled to France – was one in which both racing and driving were much encouraged, for it was said that not only did the King enjoy driving but also that he tried hard to persuade those around him to do the same.

For his coronation, however, as well as for his State entry into London the day before, he *rode* a horse. This took place on April 22nd 1661 and was described by Samuel Pepys as follows: '*So glorious was the Show with gold and silver that we were not*

17

able to look at it.' John Evelyn, too, wrote of the procession; according to his pen it was: '*Rich as embroidery, velvet, cloth-of-gold, silver, and jewells could make, as their prancing horses proceeded thro' the streetes.*' A painting still in existence proves the splendour of this occasion. It shows King Charles, wearing a tall hat trimmed with feathers and a superb gold-embroidered cape, astride a solitary snow-white charger whose mane and saddlery are completely covered with gold tassels and pom-poms. The enormously long retinue of followers, both on horseback and on foot, were similarly bedecked in crimson and gilt, which shows that the £1,000 allocated for this event was well spent.

Another painting also in existence, depicts King Charles leaving Hampton Court in a coach drawn by six black horses, which may have been a team of Friesians from Holland. It is also reported that in 1663 a French nobleman, the Chevalier de Grammont, presented the King with a coach which he had had built in France at a cost of about £1,500, and that King Charles and his Queen were later seen driving in Hyde Park in it, drawn this time by a team of six piebald horses.

Throughout his reign, coachbuilding was improving, and in 1677 King Charles granted a Charter to the Worshipful Company of Coachmakers and Coach Harnessmakers in the City of London. The Company's object was to promote the production of better carriages, providing yearly awards for '*excellence in coachmaking*'. Traffic congestion continued, however, despite the fact that the streets had been widened after the Great Fire in 1666, and, like his father before him, Charles II was forced to order a limit on the number of coaches in London.

A drawing of a coach built for King Charles II. Note that crowns have taken the place of feathers on the roof. A very similar carriage appears in a painting of King Charles II leaving Nonsuch Palace with a team of six greys, the leaders of which are driven by a postillion rider.

King James II

LIKE HIS grandfather James I, King James II had been proclaimed King of Scotland (James VII) before he came to England, which he did after the death of his brother, King Charles II, in 1685. His reign, however, lasted only three years for he fled abroad after his Dutch son-in-law, William of Orange, landed in Devon, followed him to Ireland and defeated him at the Battle of the Boyne. This short reign was mostly taken up with the Civil War, and one chronicler wrote that there was nothing worth recording about James II's excursions into London's Parks!

King William III and Queen Mary II

SINCE THE wife of William, Prince of Orange, was a daughter of the fugitive King James II, it was decided that the English throne should be shared between them, so in 1689, they were crowned together as King William III and Queen Mary II.

Mary, however, died at the early age of thirty-two in 1694, and this was also the year that King William decreed that no horses under the height of 14 hands were to be used for pulling coaches. This edict may have been issued because a previous one, dictated by King Charles I, had not been strictly adhered to, or because, on account of his Dutch nationality, William was accustomed to an altogether stronger type of horse, such as the Gelderlander and Friesian breeds, for which Holland is still known today. But at any rate this led to the production of better coach-horses in England.

In 1694, too, no less than 700 licences were issued for hackney coaches, a very big increase on the days of King Charles II, but horse-drawn transport was becoming more prolific and the streets were also being widened to deal with it.

King William III died in 1702 after having been thrown from his horse when it put its foot in a mole-hill while out hunting.

ᴄᴈ Queen Anne ᴈᴄ

QUEEN ANNE ascended to the throne in 1702 after the death of her brother-in-law, William III. Like him, she took a great interest in horses, and was a dedicated follower of hounds. She also enjoyed racing, and it was by her command that the famous course at Ascot was laid out and subsequently became known as Royal Ascot.

A painting of Queen Anne's procession to the State Opening of Parliament depicts her sitting in a small gilded State Coach, most likely fitted with glass windows. This was drawn by a team of eight grey horses, the leading pair being driven by a postillion rider, and the remaining six controlled by a coachman.

After the rich trappings shown in the picture of King Charles II's State entry into

Queen Anne driving to the State Opening of Parliament in her coach drawn by a fine team of greys. (Reproduced by gracious permission of Her Majesty The Queen)

London, it is rather surprising to see that Queen Anne's horses had unplaited manes, and that their harness, although well ornamented, appears to lack the grandeur usually associated with such an occasion. The horses, however, have both presence and quality, and it is said that during this reign there was a large number of Arabian stallions imported – which was to have a marked effect on all the lighter breeds of horses in this country.

When, on account of ill-health, she was no longer able to ride, Queen Anne followed hounds by driving herself in a chaise. It is also said that by her command, London's Hyde Park became better maintained so as to foster the sport of riding and driving.

Despite having given birth to seventeen children, twelve of whom died in childhood, Queen Anne survived them all, so that at her death in 1714, she became the last monarch of the Stuart dynasty.

King George I

WITH THE death of Queen Anne, an entirely new Royal dynasty was created by the enthronement in 1714 of King George I from Hanover – whose link with England was due to his having been a grandson of one of James I's four daughters.

King George I is said to have remained steadfastly loyal to his native Germany, even to the extent of keeping to the language. Certainly from an equine point of view, his arrival in England produced far-reaching effects by his importation of the famous cream Hanoverian horses.

These horses, which were previously venerated by the German tribes, were being bred in the Royal houses of Schaumberg-Lippe and Gotha, as well as in Hanover, for the exclusive use of the German Royal family.

At Hanover, the King had an impressive collection which comprised: some six hundred horses, including twenty teams of eight; sixteen coaches; fourteen postillions; nineteen ostlers plus farriers and stable staff. Unfortunately history does not relate how many other types of carriage there were, nor what they looked like, but one can safely guess that they were both large and very ornately decorated.

King George I's reign was to last just thirteen years for he died in 1727, but this occurred on his way home to his beloved Hanover, so that at least he was buried on German soil.

~ King George II ~

A S THE only son of George I, King George II succeeded to the throne in 1727, and remained, like his father before him, intensely patriotic to Germany. He denounced as useless, among others, English jockeys and coachmen, and added that no English horses were '*fit to be ridden, or driven*'.

Despite these criticisms he took part in many equine activities, and expenses incurred at the Royal Mews during 1740–41 amounted to over £13,000. Of this sum, his coach-maker and other tradesmen received £2,055; new liveries cost £3,928; while £1,142 went towards the purchase of horses. Also, in 1732, he commissioned the architect, William Kent, to re-build the Royal Mews at Charing Cross.

Among the King's eight children, his second daughter, the Princess Amelia, is recorded as having been the one most interested in horses; she apparently rode, and also drove a chaise. When they lived at Hampton Court Palace, the entire family used to drive to Richmond Park when the King hunted there. It was reported that in August 1728 '*Her Majesty and the Princess Amelia in a four-wheeled Chaise; the Princess Caroline in a two-wheeled Chaise, and the Princesses Mary and Louisa in a coach*' followed the hounds.

Nor was the Royal Family immune from accidents. One such mishap took place during the evening of September 17th 1739, when the King's four daughters were in a coach in Hyde Park travelling into town. A single horse chaise containing a gentleman and his daughter collided in the dusk with one the Royal leaders and turned over. The horse, its chaise and occupants were then thrown under the hooves of the Royal team of horses who, not unnaturally, '*commenced rearing, plunging, and trampling*' until four of them had also fallen down.

Eventually the screams of the Princesses attracted help and the mêlée was sorted out, but it was found that the unfortunate Royal postillion had broken both his legs, and the gentleman and his daughter were also badly hurt. No mention is made, however, of any injuries sustained by the horses, but the Princesses returned to Kensington Palace where '*they had recourse to bleeding, Eau de Carme, Eau de Luce, Hungary water, Hartshorn drops, and other fashionable composing draughts of the day, in order to restore their fluttered spirits.*'

During his reign, the famous Rotten Row (the name believed to have evolved from '*Route du Roi*') became the fashionable place in which to ride in Hyde Park, and driving there was firmly established as a pastime and spectacle for the public, which was to remain the case until the end of King Edward VII's reign – 150 years later.

Despite his early dislike of all things English, King George II appears to have eventually accepted life in England, and when he died in 1760, he became the last English King to have been buried at Westminster.

King George III

THE OLDEST and most impressive vehicle in the Royal Mews today is without doubt the Gold State Coach, which although ordered after King George III's accession to the throne in October 1760, was unfortunately not built in time for his coronation. The only State Coach available at that time was one used by Queen Anne.

Delivery of the Gold State Coach did not take place until November 24th 1762, as was recorded by the Clerk to the Royal Stables (then situated at Charing Cross). He wrote that after its arrival at 5 a.m., a team of eight cream horses were put to it, and, having found it to be '*satisfactory*', the King was able to travel in it when he attended the Opening of Parliament on the following day. The coach was further described as being '*the most superb and expensive of any ever built in this Kingdom*'.

As can be imagined, the acquisition of this magnificent vehicle – which had cost £7,661 18s 11d – caused more than average interest, and the crowd which turned out to see their monarch in his latest carriage was '*exceedingly great . . . yet no accident happened but one of the Door Glasses and the handle of the Door being broken.*'

Several designs for this coach had been submitted, and it was finally put together and built under the supervision of the Surveyor of His Majesty's Board of Works, Sir William Chambers, and although the box-seat from which a coachman could drive was later removed for King Edward VII's coronation, the Gold State Coach remains today exactly as it was built in 1762.

This huge vehicle, which weighs 4 tons, and measures 24 feet long by 8 feet 3 inches wide by 12 feet high, is gilded all over and ornate in the extreme. Its framework comprises eight palm trees supporting the roof, on which three cherubs, draped in laurel leaves and representing England, Scotland, and Ireland, hold up the Imperial Crown, as well as carrying the Sceptre, the Sword of State, and the Ensign of Knighthood.

At each of the four corners, stouter palm trees issuing from lions' heads, are decorated with trophies to symbolise Great Britain's victories in the Seven Years War. The body

A Royal Forgon. This was the vehicle used when travelling long distances to convey luggage and staff. It was sent on ahead in order to prepare for the Royal travellers. (Photo of painting by John Cordrey, courtesy of Arthur Ackermann & Son Ltd)

is slung on red leather braces with gold buckles held by four tritons – those in front having cables over their shoulders (as if pulling the vehicle) to proclaim the Monarch of the Ocean through conch-shells, while the two at the rear carry imperial fasces topped with tridents.

Other features comprise the coachman's footboard carved in the shape of a scallop-shell and decorated with bunches of marine plants; the pole made as a bundle of lances; the ornately decorated splinter-bar ending in dolphins' heads; and the wheels which are replicas of those on an ancient triumphal chariot.

In addition, the door panels – the only parts later requiring renovation due to dry rot – are covered in paintings, all of a symbolic nature, by Giovanni Battista Cipriani, an artist from Florence who came to London in 1775. Small wonder that this coach was described as *'very superb'*.

Interest in members of the Royal Family and their carriages has been recorded over the years by several writers, among them Parson James Woodforde, whose *Country Diary*, written between 1758 and 1802, remains a source of delight today. Although he resided in Norfolk, Parson Woodforde journeyed quite extensively to the southern counties, and gave endless and interesting details of life at that time. In June 1786, he describes taking Nancy, his niece, on a trip to London, where they stayed at the 'Bell Savage' [*sic*],* Ludgate Hill, and where, as they walked to Charing Cross, they met *'the Prince of Wales's carriage, with him in it.'* On the following day he recorded

---

* The Belle Sauvage at Ludgate Hill was a well-known coaching inn.

A Royal Landau (with its hood up) drawn by a team of six, followed by a mounted groom leading a spare horse, and accompanied by a pair of Dalmatian dogs which were used as guard dogs. As can be seen, the leaders are driven by a postillion rider. (Photo of painting by John Cordrey at the time of King George III, by courtesy of Arthur Ackermann & Son Ltd)

A Royal Landau (with its hood up) drawn by a four-in-hand, perhaps with King George III inside, since the two grooms in full livery are travelling on the rumble seat at the rear. (Photo of painting by John Cordrey, courtesy of Arthur Ackermann & Son Ltd)

His Majesty King George III's State Chariot, photographed when it was on display at the Great Exhibition held in Hyde Park during Queen Victoria's reign.

that he '*shewed Nancy the Mews and the King's cream coloured horses, also The King's State Coach – which she sat in.*' For this little act of *lèse-majesté* Woodforde '*gave to the men that shewed us the same – two shillings*', which was probably a reasonably handsome reward.

Another writer at this time was Fanny Burney, who, in 1786 was attached to the Court as Assistant Keeper of the Robes to Queen Charlotte. In her diary she wrote that the King himself frequently drove either his wife, or one of his daughters in a phaeton, and sometimes at considerable speed.

It was in 1784, and during the reign of King George III, that mail coaches were first introduced into England and these not only made a substantial difference to the safe delivery of mail, but they also provided a speedier and more reliable method of travel, though the fares were double those charged on road (or stage) coaches.

By the following year, an Act signed by the King was passed, which forbade the conveyance of more than six passengers on the roof of any coach, and no more than two on the box. This Act was superseded in 1790 by one which permitted only *one* person to travel on the box-seat, and no more than *four* on the roof of any coach drawn by three, or more horses, and this Law, according to paintings by contemporary artists such as James Pollard, Henry Alken, Cooper-Henderson and others, was very strictly observed on mail coaches.

It also became the custom for the coachmen of mail coaches to wear scarlet coats to match those of the Guards, in honour of the King's birthday, and certain contemporary paintings depict this also.

A white Hanoverian coach horse in a semi-State livery. Although it is described as 'white', this may well have been one of the famous cream horses introduced by King George I, which, by tradition, were only used by the monarch.

Throughout George III's reign, cream horses had been imported from Hanover, but in 1803, when Napoleon seized the town, the King became so enraged at hearing that a team of eight cream horses had been used by the Frenchman, that he decreed forthwith that only *black* horses should be used in England until Hanover was liberated. Due to their having been imported over the years, however, cream horses continued to be bred at Hampton Court until well into this century.

Due to ill-health, the last few years of King George III's life were spent in seclusion, but his reign was notable for many things, among them great improvement in transport, as well as agriculture – for which His Majesty received the nickname 'Farmer George'. He is also remembered as being the first monarch to have occupied Buckingham Palace which, as Buckingham House, he had purchased in 1762, as well as having been the provider of an outstanding carriage: the Royal Family's 'very superb' Gold State Coach.

A Royal Hanoverian coach horse in State livery.

King George IV

OF ALL Britain's monarchs, King George IV was undoubtedly the most enthu-siastic Royal 'whip', so it comes as a surprise to learn that although the Gold State Coach and team of cream-coloured horses were available, no carriages were used in his coronation procession, which he attended on foot! This may have been on account of the strained relations existing between him and his wife, Queen Caroline, for he had forbidden her to attend the ceremony, and although she tried to enter West-minster Abbey, she was turned away at the door.

The procession in 1821 lacked nothing in pageantry, however, for a wide covered platform linking the Abbey and Westminster Hall was erected three feet off the ground, and the King, who had spent the previous night at the Speaker's House nearby, walked under a splendid canopy of cloth-of-gold, wearing a twenty-seven foot long train made of crimson velvet embossed with gold stars, and was accompanied by a long retinue of gorgeously dressed attendants. After a five-hour ceremony at the Abbey, followed by a massive banquet in Westminster Hall, His Majesty eventually sank gratefully into a carriage which took him home to Carlton House.

It is as a young man, though, that King George IV first became known for his interest in driving, which was then a very popular sport. This had begun well before 1784 – the date when mail coaches were first introduced into England – but it gained momentum rapidly when young men started bribing the professional coachmen in order to learn how to drive four-in-hands – which was of course strictly against the law.

Before this date, it was customary when driving the then currently fashionable high phaetons which could be drawn by four, six, or eight horses, for the leaders to be ridden by postillions, but this method was potentially very dangerous (as Oliver Crom-well had discovered to his cost) for, if a postillion rider were to fall off, then the driver, with only the reins of the wheelers in his hands, was powerless to control the team. Since the young Prince and his friends often drove this type of turnout, a safety device was invented consisting of a lever which, when pressed by foot from the box-seat, could open the pole-hook and thus release the leaders, and at least two engravings depicting this device were printed.

In addition to driving, the Prince also took a very active interest in the construction

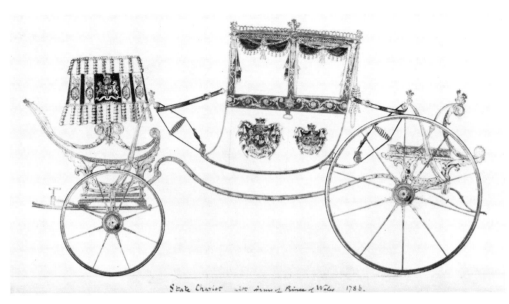

State Chariot with arms of Prince of Wales 1786.

An exquisite example of a coachmaker's art – a drawing of a State Chariot designed by William Cook for the Prince of Wales (later King George IV).

This unusual print, believed to be a portrait of Lady Lade, who with her husband, Sir John, was a friend of the Prince of Wales, depicts a safety device which was invented in case a postillion rider fell off, when of course, the team would have been uncontrollable. By pressing a pedal on the foot-board, the pole-hook could be opened to release the bars to which the leading horses were attached. The leaders having galloped off, the wheelers could be driven in safety.

A design for a High Crane-neck Phaeton for the Prince of Wales (later King George IV). This type of vehicle was known as a 'Highflyer' — the crane-neck type of perch undercarriage having been built with an arch so that the front wheels could turn under when going round corners.

A drawing, signed by William Cook of Liquorpond Street, of a slightly lower-built Crane-neck Phaeton designed for the Prince of Wales when he had become Regent.

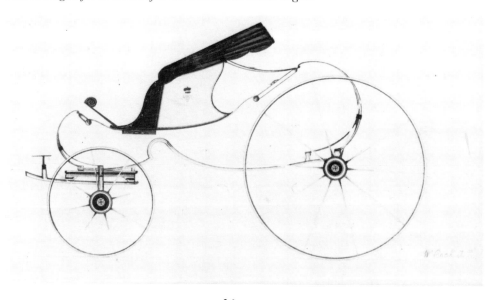

of his carriages, discussing them so frequently with his coachbuilder, William Cook of Liquorpond Street, that the latter is said to have been nicknamed 'King' Cook by his contemporaries. Three of Cook's exquisite drawings, consisting of two Royal Phaetons and a State Chariot, are still in existence. In 1783, the year of his twenty-first birthday, when he was created Prince of Wales, a new and beautiful State Coach was built, and this was used for his first official attendance at the Opening of Parliament when, as Prince of Wales, he took his seat in the House of Lords.

1783 was also the year when the Prince of Wales moved into Carlton House. Although it was said that his extravagance forced him by 1786 to close this house and to sell his horses and carriages, the following year he was offering to buy five grey ponies at twelve guineas each from Sir John Lade, and by 1790, was again installed in Carlton House.

Sir John Lade and his wife, Letty, were both expert 'whips', and the Prince's friendship with them is well documented. The letters which passed between them – now in the Royal Archives – are of absorbing interest as they record the surprising length of journeys undertaken at this time. Writing from Carlton House to Sir John Lade in 1791 the Prince said:

> *'You asked me when it would be likely for me to be at Bagshot. I mean to be there at one o'clock tomorrow. I shall come down in ye Curricle and shall drive back again after an early dinner. If it should suit you to meet me there and afterwards to return to Town in the Curricle I shall be very glad of the pleasure of your company.'*

Even at a fast trot averaging about 12 m.p.h. this journey of approximately twenty-eight miles must have taken over two hours each way.

For these excursions the Prince had invested in the vehicle referred to – the Curricle – which held two people only, and was unusual in that despite its having only two wheels, it was drawn by a *pair* of horses, the weight of the pole between them being borne by a steel bar attached to the pads on their backs. Originating in Italy, where it was ideal for traversing rough roads, it was the fastest moving vehicle available, and therefore immensely popular with young men. The name is believed to have been evolved from '*currus*' – a mountain goat.

Although the roads at this time had not yet been perfected by the engineers Telford and Macadam, the main coaching routes out of London were passable, and in addition to visiting Bagshot, the Prince of Wales often drove on to Kempshot Park near Basingstoke, and then home to either Carlton House or Windsor Castle. It is the Brighton road, however, which is most associated with the Prince's driving exploits, for it has been widely reported that he once drove a '*randem*' (three horses one behind the other) down this road. Sadly, this event never appears to have been recorded pictorially, but there is an engraving depicting him at the reins of his Curricle on this road with, as was customary when there was no rumble seat at the rear of the vehicle, two grooms

The Prince Regent on the road to Brighton with his Curricle – the only two-wheeled vehicle in England built to take a pair *of horses. Note the two grooms in Royal livery riding behind.*

dressed in Royal livery riding behind.

Brighton, or 'Brighthelmstone' as it was then called, always held a great fascination for the Prince of Wales. Visiting it in 1784 when he was aged twenty-two, he bought a small farmhouse on whose site he later had built the now famous Pavilion, but in 1808, ten years before this was completed, he had a vast and sumptuously-decorated stable block put up at the enormous cost of £70,000. As one contemporary writer put it: '*At least his horses are in a Palace, even if he is living in a cottage.*' Palace it certainly was, as described in 1825:

> '*The exterior is of octagonal form, but the interior is a circle, inclosing an area of about 25 feet in circumference. This is surmounted by a vast dome, from which the whole is lighted by large, glazed compartments. The stables, sixty-two in number, surround the area, and are so disposed that, when the doors are open, a spectator standing beneath the centre of the dome may view the interior of every stall without moving from his situation. Over the stables are numerous apartments for grooms etc. which open from a light gallery going round the circle. On the south side, a spacious arch, similar to the northern entrance, opens to the Pavilion grounds, and corresponding arches to the east and west communicate with a tennis court and riding school.*'

Known today as 'The Dome', the stable block is now used for conferences, lectures and concerts, as it holds up to two thousand people, while the riding school can seat over a thousand for a meal.

King George IV

The welfare of his horses was always one of the Prince's main concerns, for in another letter to Sir John Lade he wrote: *'My poor chestnut horse I rode the first stage yesterday, died last night.'* Whether or not this was as a result of the many attempts at speed-breaking records, which were indulged in at that time, is not known, but Thackeray is quoted as having written: *'Where my Prince did actually distinguish himself was in driving. Once he drove in four hours and a half from Brighton to Carlton House – fifty-six miles.'* This was not far off the time achieved in 1888 by Jim Selby, when he made his record-breaking coach drive from Piccadilly to Brighton and back in under eight hours.

Although Brighton appears to have been the Prince's favourite resort, he also visited Bath, presumably to 'take the waters' there. In April 1793 he wrote that he was *'just stepping into my Chaise to return to Bath'* after having been *'very ill indeed'*. The chaise referred to would have been his Travelling Chariot, or Post Chaise, drawn by a team of four, or perhaps six horses with postillion riders.

As befitted an heir apparent, the future King had homes in many different parts of the country. Windsor Castle was one, and a convenient 'stepping-stone' when visit-

Detail from an engraving of an aquatint by John Bodger which shows the Prince of Wales (later King George IV) at the reins of his Highflyer Phaeton on Newmarket Heath. The similar phaeton on the left is said to have belonged to friends of the Prince, Lord Barrymore and his sister.

ing his friends, the Lades, at their house in Taplow.

The Prince also went to Newmarket to attend the races and to sit in his Highflyer Phaeton and watch his horses in training on the Heath. John Bodger chose this site for an aquatint which shows the Prince and his friends, the Barrymores, in this type of vehicle. His Highflyer Phaeton was also depicted in an engraving of him driving '*a lady of quality to Ascot*', as well as in a painting by George Stubbs, which has a smart pair of black horses in harness waiting to be put to, while the head coachman and a groom busy themselves on the ground. This picture, which displays well the extreme height of this most elegant type of carriage, remains in The Queen's collection at Windsor, and has been reproduced as a coloured print.

Newmarket, too, was where Tattersalls held their auction sales, at which the Prince occasionally entered horses. In a letter written in April 1793, he told Sir John Lade that he had '*pledged on his honour*' to offer for sale there a horse for 250 guineas, but that if it failed to reach that figure, he had promised it to a gentleman for 200 guineas, adding that this price was much more than he could '*possibly think of giving for any pair of horses*'. His letter proceeds with an offer to Sir John of 130 guineas for two horses, which he said he could not consider purchasing until he had driven them. The Prince, clearly, bought sensibly.

Over the years, the Prince of Wales had been putting on weight, and before 1815, when he became Regent, he had given up riding. But climbing up into high vehicles had also become a problem, and so, by the time he attained the throne, a new and low-slung carriage had been produced for him, which was to oust the fashion for Highflyers. This was modelled on the lines of the pony phaetons built for ladies, children, and invalids. It has been recorded that when his daughter, the Princess Charlotte, was expecting her baby, she drove about the grounds of Claremont, her home in Surrey, in a low pony chaise.

The King obviously delighted in his new little carriage drawn by a very smart pair of ponies, and one or two engravings were made showing him at their reins. It was in this small phaeton that Queen Victoria met him driving through the grounds at Windsor when, in 1827 as a little girl, she visited the Castle. This so impressed her that she mentioned it in her journal.

Once he was monarch, King George IV lost no time in planning State visits, for only a few days after his coronation he set sail for Ireland from Portsmouth, obviously preferring the possible rigours of a longer sea journey to the jolting on rough roads across country to Holyhead. The death meanwhile of his estranged wife, Queen Caroline, did not – or perhaps it might be more accurate to say *could* not – affect his plans. After landing in Ireland he spent a quiet five-day period in mourning before making a ceremonial entry into Dublin on August 17th.

For this visit the King had brought his own fleet of carriages, which included his State Coach whose roof was now embellished with a crown instead of three feathers.

King George IV travelling in one of his chariots in Hyde Park. Driven by postillion riders, with out-riders in front, two mounted grooms at the back, and a groom on the rumble-seat, His Majesty was well protected. (Painted by James Pollard, and reproduced by courtesy of N.C. Selway, author of The Golden Age of Coaching and Sport)

An early engraving of the Prince of Wales (later King George IV) driving a lady of quality to Ascot. The drawing of the Highflyer Phaeton is not, however, very accurate, for the hoops in the two crane-neck perches are depicted too far back to be able to accommodate the front wheels when turning. (Picture from Radio Times Hulton Picture Library)

An engraving of King George IV driving his low pony phaeton. This was built during his later years when he found that his increasing age and girth made climbing into high vehicles a difficulty. Queen Victoria recorded driving with him in this type of carriage when she was a little girl.

Perhaps in deference to his wife's death, this vehicle was left empty and the King travelled behind it in an open Landau, standing up alone with his arms folded across his chest. Dressed in full military regalia, but with a wide black mourning band round one arm, His Majesty completely captured the hearts of the Irish by wearing a large sprig of Shamrock inserted into his cocked hat.

During his nine years on the throne, King George IV was the instigator of several new developments and customs, one being the transference in 1825 of the Royal Mews from Charing Cross to its present site in the grounds of Buckingham Palace, into which he had moved after his coronation. Although some stables already existed there, he commissioned the architect John Nash to redesign the whole area and it was built as it stands today.

Nash was also asked to produce drawings for the Royal Stand at Ascot, and it was here that the King inaugurated the now annual custom for the Royal Family to drive down the course in open carriages. This was clearly very popular with the public as described on June 3rd 1825 by Thomas Creevey:

'We saw "Prinney" looking quite as well, and nearly as merry as we have seen him in his best days. Contrary to his former practice, he drove up the Course to his stand, in the presence of everybody – himself in the first coach and four, the Duke of Wellington sitting by his side. There were three other carriages and four, and a phaeton after him, and I sh'd think 20 servants in scarlet on horseback, and all his horses are of the greatest beauty, the whole thing looked very splendid; in short, quite as it should be.'

Although Creevey referred to the King as '*Prinney*' when he had in fact been crowned four years previously, it was clearly an affectionate nickname, for two years later, and having in the same sentence mentioned '*the Monarch*' he again describes '*Prinney*' driving his phaeton at Ascot. By 1828, however, Creevey recorded that at Ascot on June 4th:

> '*It was a pleasure to see our beloved Sovereign enjoy it as he seemed to do, and I never saw him look better in all my life. He drove up the course with little George Cumberland by his side, with 7 carriages and 31 outriders, besides footmen seated behind the carriages.*'

During the King's lifetime, his taste in carriages was always avidly copied, and many improvements in their design and construction achieved. His special interest in them also heralded an upsurge in the art of driving, and this, together with the establishment of an efficient postal system by coach, led to Telford and Macadam's inventions for new and better road surfaces.

The death in 1830 of King George IV at Windsor Castle, ended a life which had been both colourful and sad, and although no horses had attended his coronation at least there were some at his funeral.

King William IV

AFTER THE pedestrian coronation of his late brother, George IV, it comes as a surprise to learn that King William IV, who was always known as the Sailor King, had the largest attendance of carriages at his procession – no less than twenty-two having been on parade, and these are depicted in a long frieze hanging in the Royal Mews. His Majesty was also the first monarch to have used his father's impressive Gold State Coach and team of cream horses on this historic occasion.

By tradition, the Royal horses never went out with manes unplaited – crimson being the colour of the ribbons used with the black horses, while purple was reserved for the creams. On one occasion, however, it was recorded that King William IV, one of whose traits was apparently a dislike of pomp and ceremony, succeeded in dispensing with this tradition and managed to appear in public with a team whose manes billowed in the wind.

This occurred in 1831, when Earl Grey and Lord Brougham had called to recommend an early dissolution of Parliament, and the King, upon impulse, decided to set

King William IV driving near Windsor Castle in his Chariot, again with postillion riders, four grooms riding fore and aft (His Majesty was known as the Sailor King*) and two grooms on the rumble-seat. The grooms are all indicating that they are about to turn right. (Painted by James Pollard, and reproduced by courtesy of N.C. Selway, from his book* The Golden Age of Coaching and Sport*)*

out at once. On being told that this would not leave sufficient time for plaiting, His Majesty retorted with some asperity: '*Plait their manes?*', followed by what was described as '*the loudest and of course most dignified of expletives*'. He then threatened to '*go in a Hackney coach*', and thus managed to flout a Royal custom.

Flouting a custom was one thing but His Majesty's impetuous decision nearly resulted in an accident. The Creams, not having been sufficiently exercised , were fresh, and when hurriedly harnessed and then driven by an enraged coachman, they behaved appallingly. First shying at a detachment of saluting guardsmen, they then succeeded in breaking into a brisk trot. A contemporary writer recorded that '*His Majesty proceeded at a faster rate than usual in his eagerness to carry out the wishes of his people*' and that he arrived at the Houses of Parliament well ahead of time.

It was fortunate that the Head Coachman, Mr Roberts, managed to hold the team, but, after having deposited his Royal Master, he was then forced to dismount from the box in order to apologise to the Guards for his unseemly language to them. '*If he had not done so'*, the same historian recounted, *'it was more than probable that the King would have had to have called a Hackney coach for his return journey, as the unplaited team would have gone home coachmanless.'*

Despite King William's leanings towards the sea, as a young man he displayed great pleasure in the acquisition of new carriages. In her diary Fanny Burney recounts that at Kew *'some talk then ensued upon the Duke's [of Clarence] new carriage – which all agreed to be the most beautiful that day at Court'* and that as she had not seen it, he had invited her to do so.

King William's reign was terminated by his death in 1837 after only six years on the throne, but his widow, Queen Adelaide, contributed to the history of Royal carriages by presenting Queen Victoria's children with a miniature Barouche. This enchanting little vehicle, which could be drawn by small pony or a donkey, was built by Corben of Twickenham in 1846, and it so delighted its recipients that Queen Victoria mentioned it in her journal.

∽ *Queen Victoria* ∾

QUEEN VICTORIA'S accession to the throne in 1837 heralded an upsurge in the design of coachbuilding, which was to reach its peak at the time of the Great Exhibition in 1851. In 1838, the year of her coronation, a new State Landau had been built for her, but for the coronation procession, the Gold State Coach was of course produced to convey her from Buckingham Palace – into which she had moved the previous July – for the ceremony at Westminster Abbey.

The day before, on June 27th, a rehearsal had been arranged, when the Queen drove to the Abbey in an open Landau, in order to see the preparations and to try out sitting on the two thrones. Finally, on June 28th, and at 10 a.m. precisely, the young Queen got into the magnificent Gold State Coach, drawn by a team of eight cream horses, to attend this historic event.

Until recently, when it was re-upholstered with modern materials, the Gold State Coach had never been renowned for its comfort, and this occasion apparently proved no exception. Although Queen Victoria did travel in it later that year to dine with the Lord Mayor at the Mansion House, on subsequent celebrations, such as her wedding, and both her golden and diamond jubilees, she preferred to use the open State Landau.

From an early age, Queen Victoria appears to have taken a great interest in her horses and carriages, judging from the many references made to them throughout her journal. This may have started when, on her seventh birthday, she is said to have been given a beautifully matched pair of Shetland ponies with exquisite harness, and a low phaeton big enough for herself and a governess. The vehicle was driven by a postillion rider wearing *a neat livery of green and gold, with a black velvet cap.*

The following year, when she was eight, she and her mother, the Duchess of Kent, went to stay at Windsor Castle with her uncle, King George IV, whom they encountered driving his low phaeton, accompanied by the Duchess of Gloucester. This event she recorded as follows:

> *'and he said 'Pop her in,' and I was lifted in and placed between him and Aunt Gloucester, who held me round the waist. (Mama was much frightened.) I was greatly pleased. . . . We drove round the nicest part of Virginia Water and stopped at the Fishing Temple . . .'*

Later, when asked what she had enjoyed most during her stay at Windsor, the little Princess is said to have replied: *'The drive I took with you, Uncle King,'* which must, of course, have delighted His Majesty.

In 1832, when she was thirteen, Princess Victoria accompanied her mother on a three-month tour of the country, beginning in Wales. Her enjoyment in her journeys was evident from the detailed descriptions in her diary about the many changes of horses.

The start from Kensington Palace in London on August 1st was early, soon after 7 a.m. Having changed horses at Barnet, St Albans and Dunstable, they reached Towcester by 1.30 p.m. Lunch here was a speedy affair for they set off again at 2.14 p.m., with more changes of horses at Daventry, Dunchurch and Coventry, until at 5.30 p.m., they reached Meridon, where they lodged *at a very clean inn.*

The following morning they were up at 5 a.m. to leave by 7.30 and changed horses at Birmingham. After lunching at Shrewsbury, the Princess recorded that they left at 2.45 p.m., and that their horses were *watered half-way* to Welshpool, where they were escorted by a troop of Yeomanry to the castle belonging to Lord Powis, with whom they stayed.

A week later, the young Princess and her mother drove to Carnarvon, and wrote that her cousins *sat on the box* of their carriage.

After having stayed with the Marquess of Anglesey at Plas Newydd, they then drove on into Cheshire for a visit to the Marquess of Westminster,* who *sent his own fine horses, which were put to our carriage* for the final stage to Eaton Hall. Whilst there, the Princess recorded going out for a drive round the estate with Lady Westminster and her eldest daughter.

*Dukedom created in 1874.

Princess Victoria in her little pony phaeton at Windsor with a team of four driven by postillion riders.

Their next visit took place on October 19th and was to the Duke of Devonshire at Chatsworth. There she visited the stables and saw '*some pretty ponies and a Russian coachman in his full dress*', and, after luncheon, drove '*with the Duke and Mrs Cavendish, in a carriage and six*' on a local sight-seeing tour.

November 7th found them in Oxfordshire, and changing horses at Woodstock, when, accompanied by a detachment of Yeomanry, they went to stay at Wytham Abbey, the seat of Lord Abingdon.

The following day a visit to the University of Oxford was made '*in a close carriage and four with Lord Abingdon and Lady Charlotte Bertie, the other ladies going in a carriage before us.*' This journey ended on Friday, November 9th, when they returned to Kensington Palace, at 5.30 p.m.

The following summer a trip on their yacht *Emerald* entailed driving to Portsmouth, and was preceded by the usual early start at 7 a.m. By now Princess Victoria had learned to differentiate between the types of carriage, and so we read that the cavalcade consisted of: '*Sir John [Conroy] going in a post-chaise before us, then our post-chaise, the Lehzen's landau, then my cousin's carriage, then Charles's, then Lady Conroy's, and then our maids.*'

In 1834, the Princess visited East Sussex and Kent, and a contemporary engraving depicts the Royal party leaving Tunbridge Wells in two Post Chaises and a closed

Landau. While staying at St Leonards, she describes setting out in a Barouche with Lady Flora Hastings and Baroness Lehzen, but that when they decided to walk, they sent the Barouche home. Later, however, they got into *'the close [sic] Landau with postillion and horse in-hand'* and became involved in what might have been a serious accident. As they approached the town

> *'the hand-horse kicked up and, getting entangled in the traces, fell down, pulling the other with it; the horse with the postillion however instantly recovered itself, but the other horse remained on the ground kicking and struggling most violently. Two gentlemen very civilly came and held the horse's head down while we all got out as fast as possible. I called for poor dear little Dashy* who was in the rumble; Wood (our footman) took him down and I ran on with him in my arms calling Mama to follow, Lehzen and Lady Flora followed us also. They then cut the traces, the horse still struggling violently. The other horse which had been quite quiet, being frightened by the other's kicking, backed and fell over into a foundation pit, while Wood held him, and he (Wood) with difficulty prevented himself from falling: the horse recovering himself ran after us and we instantly ran behind a stone wall; but the horse went along the road, and a workman took him and gave him to Wood. The other horse had ceased kicking and got up.*
>
> *We ought to be most grateful to Almighty God for His merciful providence in thus preserving us, for it was a very narrow escape. The names of the two gentlemen who held the horse's head are Rev. Mr Gould and Mr Peckham Micklethwaite. The latter I am sorry to say was hurt, but not very materially. The poor horse is cut from head to foot; but the other is not at all hurt only very much frightened. We walked home . . .'*

More tours were made in 1835, and on one, when she reached King's Lynn, the Princess's popularity was such that the inhabitants insisted upon removing the horses, and themselves pulling her carriage to the inn at which she was to stay.

In November 1836, Princess Victoria visited Canterbury, but recorded that they encountered a violent storm: *'a hurricane, for I cannot call it by any other name'*, and that *'our carriage swung and the postboys could scarcely keep on their horses'*. So strong was the wind, that after reaching Sittingbourne she and her mother transferred themselves into the carriage occupied by Lady Theresa Fox-Strangways and Baroness Lehzen *'which, being larger and heavier than our post-chaise, would not shake so much'*. This, however, did not altogether solve the problem, for at one moment the horses came to a halt, *'but by dint of whipping and very good management of the postboys, we reached Rochester in safety'* where, since *'a coach had upset on the bridge, and the battlements were totally blown in'*, they were forced to spend the night.

* Her little dog.

A design for a new phaeton for Her Majesty Queen Victoria. (Reproduced by courtesy of Radio Times Hulton Library)

The following year, Princess Victoria ascended to the throne and during 1838, the year of her coronation, a State Landau was built for her, and this is still in use at the Royal Mews. The railway had by now started to cast its network over England, and official visits began to be made by this new and speedier form of travel. The Royal carriages therefore ceased being built to withstand rough roads or for carrying quantities of luggage.

A great deal of interest was naturally taken in Queen Victoria's possessions – which of course included her carriages – and in 1840, the year of her marriage to Prince Albert, a new phaeton, which she could drive herself, was produced, and a drawing of it was published in *The Literary World*. Two years later, Barker & Co. built the large and impressive-looking Ivory-mounted Phaeton, another vehicle which is occasionally used today.

Although this carriage, with its elegantly curved lines, may have been intended for the Queen herself to drive it is doubtful that she could have done so. The dashboard (or 'splasher') was built, like many others at that time, of a height to hide from view the horses' posteriors, but in fact it was so lofty that only their ears were visible from the driving seat. On account of this, together with the overall size, it is more likely that this phaeton, designed to take large horses, was intended for either a pair or a team of four driven by postillion riders.

Despite the extra burdens of work caused by sovereignty and marriage, Queen Victoria continued to record descriptions of journeys and carriages in her journal. In 1843, when she and Prince Albert visited King Louis-Philippe of France at the Chateau d'Eu, she recorded that they set off for a picnic luncheon in the forest *'with the whole company*

Prince Albert is said to have introduced sleighs into the Royal Mews, and is here seen driving Queen Victoria, a governess, and one of the children at Brighton. Note that ostrich plumes, which were used on Queen Elizabeth I's coaches and then subsequently only on funeral carriages, appear to have been re-introduced here.

in char-à-bancs. Albert sitting in front with the King, then I with the Queen . . . and behind us Louise and the other Princesses'.

This excursion in a vehicle capable of carrying such a large party *en famille* appears to have delighted Queen Victoria so much that the following year, when the French King made a State visit to England, he brought with him a similar char-à-banc to present to her. This vehicle, built by Gautier et Picheron of Paris, was used for shooting parties, and its arrival at Windsor is depicted in a watercolour by Joseph Nash.

Like many of the Queen's carriages, the char-à-banc was copied extensively, and became so popular that a similar, though smaller carriage, the Wagonette – which could be used for transporting a fewer number of people on country outings – came into being. In 1845 Hoopers built one for Queen Victoria under the personal supervision of the Prince Consort. This was also copied and widely used by Victorian families for shooting parties and other country pursuits.

A family outing at Osborne on the Isle of Wight. Queen Victoria accompanying her children, with Prince Edward (later King Edward VII) driving a pair of goats to a miniature Siamese phaeton. The driving of goats remained a popular pastime for children until the beginning of this century.

Queen Victoria appears always to have been an active and enthusiastic 'whip', as was Prince Albert who is said to have introduced horse-drawn sleighs into the Royal Mews. The most impressive of these was designed by the Prince himself. In February 1845, while staying at the Pavilion in Brighton, the Queen wrote in her journal:

> '*It had been snowing all night. . . . Albert tried out our pretty smart sledge, which made him rather late for luncheon. At 3 o'clock we went out in it together and I thought it quite charming. Meyer sat on the place behind, a sort of saddle with two places for the feet, one on either side. The horses with their handsome red harness and many bells had a charming effect. Albert drove from the seat and we went along the London road . . . and the sledge went delightfully though the road was unfortunately very much broken up in places but in others it was covered with snow . . .*'

Another similar outing, at Windsor, was described by a Royal governess:

This enchanting little donkey-sized barouche (although seen here put to a Shetland pony) was given to Queen Victoria's children by Queen Adelaide, the widowed Consort of King William IV. (Reproduced by gracious permission of Her Majesty The Queen)

'*This morning we had a very pretty and brilliant amusement. The Queen took the Princess Royal, with me to hold her, in the sledge, the Prince driving. The sledge is quite pretty: beautiful grey ponies all covered with bells and sparkling harness. The gentlemen attending, and scarlet-coated grooms preceding and following, over the dazzling snow in the purest sunshine.*'

Queen Victoria's children were clearly encouraged to drive, as is shown in an attractive engraving which depicts the little Prince Edward (later King Edward VII) at the reins of a pair of goats harnessed to a miniature Siamese phaeton – which was so named on account of its 'twin' seats, one behind the other. The driving of goats, either singly or in pairs, was a popular pastime for children until well into the Edwardian era, but for safety's sake, a groom, as in this picture, or some other person was invariably required to hold an additional rein in order to control the animals if need be.

In 1846, Queen Adelaide, the widowed Queen Consort of King William IV, commissioned Corben of Twickenham to build a miniature barouche. This she gave to the Royal children as a Christmas present that year. This enchanting little carriage could be drawn by either a donkey or small pony, and it gave such pleasure that Queen Victoria recorded the following words in her journal:

'*After luncheon, the five children were in the greatest delight over a little miniature barouche, with a box for a coachman, and a place for a footman, which the Queen Dowager has given them. The three girls seated themselves inside, while the two boys sat, the one on the box, and the other standing up behind, the gentlemen dragging the carriage up and down the corridor to their intense joy.'*

This little vehicle survived to delight further generations of Royal children and is on view to the public in the Royal Mews.

Although she was accustomed to travelling in large and rather imposing vehicles, Queen Victoria was also interested in the smaller and more ordinary types. For instance, in 1849 when she paid her first State visit to Ireland she recorded seeing people in traditional Irish jaunting cars.

After going to Dublin – where she was met by her own carriages with postillion riders in their Ascot liveries – she described a drive to a local beauty spot which commanded an extensive view of the Wicklow Hills. Here, she got out and

'walked across a little wooden bridge to a very pretty cottage. We drove back in a Jaunting car, which is a double one with four wheels, and held a number of us. I, sitting on one side between Albert and the Duke [of Leinster]; the Duchess, Lady Jocelyn, Lord Clarendon and Lady Waterford on the opposite side. George [Prince George] at the back, and the equerries on either side of the coachman.'

The traditional Irish jaunting (or side-) car was always built with only two wheels and to hold no more than *five* people, so it is interesting that Queen Victoria not only noted the number of wheels and that it held eleven passengers, but also that she referred to it as a 'double' jaunting car. This vehicle may have been one of the many built by Bianconi, an Italian who, from a very humble beginning, eventually made his fortune in Ireland by introducing a public transport system between the towns. For this he evolved larger-sized jaunting cars with four wheels, to be pulled by pairs and even teams of four horses, and these cars eventually bore his name.

It was during Queen Victoria's reign that the coachbuilding industry reached its zenith of perfection. Previously, carriages had been rather clumsily built, but with the rapid improvement in road surfaces, together with the fact that many women followed the lead set by the Queen and drove themselves, vehicles, even the larger ones intended for professional coachmen to drive, became constructed upon more delicate lines.

The Great Exhibition, which was staged in Hyde Park in 1851 at the instigation of the Prince Consort, saw the ultimate in coachbuilding. Some of the designs contained in its catalogue – described as being *'of unsurpassed elegance'* – were fanciful in the extreme. There were phaetons, for instance, with bodies shaped like nautilus shells, their ironwork ending in scrolls; and ornately decorated barouches containing canework panels, with ormolu-encrusted lamps which were further enhanced by delicate tracings of frosted glass.

Royal Cavalcade

Queen Victoria herself was impressed by the standard of the many and varied exhibits. On April 29th, accompanied by only two maids of honour and two equerries, she drove to it for a private view that lasted two hours and recorded in her diary that she returned *'quite dead beat and my head really bewildered by the myriads of beautiful and wonderful things.'*.

The official opening of the Exhibition took place on May 1st, which Queen Victoria performed after having arrived with a procession of no less than nine State carriages, and she described the event as: *'one of the greatest and most glorious days of our lives, with which to my pride and joy, the name of my beloved Albert is forever associated . . .'* Thereafter, the Great Exhibition became a mecca, not only for everyone in the British Isles, but also for a great many visitors from abroad. Its display of English-built carriages brought forth the comment that 'British coachbuilding was the envy of the world'.

Two years later a similar exhibition was staged in Dublin. In order to encourage Irish industry, as well as, perhaps, to compare it with the one held in London, the Queen and Prince Albert immediately paid a visit. On display was a State coach built by a Mr Hutton, a coachbuilder who was also the Lord Mayor of Dublin. The vehicle was both elegant and ornate, with gilt metal scroll-work on the roof and a matching design painted on the panels beneath the windows. Queen Victoria was so impressed with this coach that she bought it. With the additions of a golden crown on the roof

The Gold State Coach as it was when used by Queen Victoria for her Coronation. The very ornate hammercloth covering the box-seat was removed for the coronation of her son, King Edward VII, and this coach has been drawn by a team of eight with four postillion riders ever since.

The 'very superb' Gold State Coach which was built for King George III in 1762 and is still used today. (Photo: Jim Bennett, Alpha)

The phaeton and horses belonging to the Prince of Wales (later King George IV), from a painting by George Stubbs. This demonstrates the extreme height of a Highflyer Phaeton. (Reproduced by gracious permission of Her Majesty The Queen)

Queen Victoria in her ivory-mounted phaeton at a meet of harriers. A painting by Henry Barraud, 1845. This carriage was used by our present Queen in 1987 when she gave up riding to the Trooping of the Colour.

Outside Windsor Castle, Queen Victoria and King Louis-Philippe of France in the char-à-banc which he presented to her in 1844. From a painting by Joseph Nash. (Reproduced by gracious permission of Her Majesty The Queen)

This small State coach is in fact the one now known as the Irish State Coach, which Queen Victoria saw in Dublin and subsequently purchased. It is still used today for important occasions of State.

and the Royal heraldic bearings painted on the door panels, it became known as the Irish State Coach, and was considered the second most important carriage in the Royal Mews, a position it holds there to this day.

In addition to the many large and impressive-looking carriages which were kept for the Queen's use at her various abodes, she owned several small vehicles. One, a pony-sized chair-back gig, had been on display at the Great Exhibition, when it was described as: '*Her Majesty's first carriage*'. This she had probably used for excursions around her estates, but in 1851, a Mr Richard Andrews, a coachbuilder who was also the Mayor of Southampton, was commanded to build another little vehicle – a pony phaeton, for use at Osborne, on the Isle of Wight.

Conscious of the honour bestowed by Royal patronage, Mr Andrews requested that he might be allowed to deliver his little phaeton in person. When, however, he did so, members of the Queen's entourage were somewhat taken aback at seeing him approach her – much as he would have any other customer – saying: '*Get into it Your Majesty, and see how you like it,*' which was followed by his unceremoniously tucking in her skirt with the words; '*There! You're in as nice a little carriage as ever you sat in.*'

The Queen, however, accepted his remarks with her usual equanimity, and Mr Andrews later received a message to the effect that Her Majesty and the Prince had

A single-seated little chair-back gig which belonged to Queen Victoria, and was on view to the public at the Great Exhibition held in 1851.

expressed '*their entire satisfaction with the style, elegance, and extraordinary lightness and construction of the carriage*' – which in fact weighed scarcely three hundredweight. This little vehicle, the front wheels of which measure only eighteen inches, while those of the rear are a mere thirty inches in height, was used extensively by Queen Victoria and is in the Royal Mews today.

Queen Victoria appears to have enjoyed driving herself about, and was undoubtedly the possessor of that mystical and often unattainable quality known as 'good hands', for she was complimented upon her driving in a contemporary magazine entitled *The Road*, which reported that '*Her Majesty is extremely gentle in handling the reins, and coaxes her steeds more by the lips than the whip.*' Nevertheless she was involved in one or two accidents, being thrown out when her pony chaise hit the side of a mole-hill on one occasion, and sprained her thumb when her carriage overturned at a meet of hounds on another. Her greatest anxiety, however, occurred when Prince Albert narrowly escaped serious injury when the team of four drawing the carriage in which she was travelling, bolted. Luckily he managed to jump clear before they collided with a wagon at a railway crossing.

This accident, in which one of the horses was killed and the coachman badly injured, caused only superficial cuts to Prince Albert's face, and the Queen recorded her gratitude to the Almighty for her husband's escape from more serious harm.

The welfare of horses also always claimed Queen Victoria's attention, as is proved in an account of a visit she and her family paid to France in 1857. After arriving at Cherbourg on August 19th she wrote that they were driven out into the country in an open char-à-banc drawn by four horses in the fashion she described as: '*the regular French poste – driven by one postillion on the wheel-horse, harnessed with ropes, no springs to the carriage, so that we bumped along pretty roughly . . .*'

After about fourteen miles, which included several steep hills, they arrived at the little town of Bucquebec. Here they set out to explore the place on foot as there were '*very tired horses to feed*'. On their return to the stables, however, Queen Victoria was concerned to find that in her opinion the horses were not sufficiently rested. Despite fearing that it would make them late for a dinner party aboard the Royal Yacht, she delayed her departure and they did not start back for Cherbourg until nearly 7 o'clock.

Horses formed an important part of Queen Victoria's life and a contemporary writer stated that in the Royal Mews in London there were from ninety to a hundred horses, comprising:

'*State horses; harness horses; coach, and light; riding horses, and what not. . . . The state stables, for the creams and blacks, are on the north side, and to the left of them are housed the thirty-two splendid bays, many of them bred at the Queen's stud farms at Hampton Court. . . . Of a different class altogether are the "State horses", which appear only on procession days, and are as much a part of the pageantry of royalty as the crown and sceptre. . . . These have a stable to themselves, the "creams" on one side, the "blacks" on the other. The creams, like the dynasty, are of Hanoverian origin, but they have for generations been of British birth, and being either entire horses or mares, they require a good deal of attention. . . . Opposite to them are the blacks, which though perhaps not so graceful, are more serviceable-looking. They are also of Hanoverian origin, being essentially well-bred specimens of the better class of hearse-horse, now rare amongst us owing to the preference given by our undertakers to the more sympathetically lugubrious (and cheaper) Flemish breed. . . .*'

A Cleveland Bay carriage-horse wearing State harness.

Queen Victoria, surrounded by some of her children, at the reins of a cream-coloured pony which, being a smaller edition of her famous cream horses, gave her immense pleasure. She is seen here with a very elegant lady's phaeton. (Reproduced by gracious permission of Her Majesty The Queen)

This reference to 'Flemish' horses probably meant the Dutch all-black breed of Friesians, which are still bred in Holland and are outstandingly good movers. More stockily built than Hanoverians, they were extensively imported at that time for funeral purposes. At least one large firm of London undertakers, however, owned a beautiful team of black horses which they proudly advertised as having come from 'Her Majesty's stable', and which, judging from a photograph of them drawing a hearse, look impressive enough to have been Hanoverians from the Royal Mews, yet the same contemporary writer stated categorically that none of the Royal horses were ever disposed of outside, except to the Life Guards, and this was most likely to be true.

The Royal teams of black horses always had their manes plaited with crimson-coloured ribbons, while purple was used for the creams. Since the creams were never used for anyone other than the Sovereign, they were undoubtedly among Queen Victoria's favourites, for when she was presented with a little cream-coloured pony, as being a miniature of her larger horses, several photographs prove that she drove it extensively.

After the tragically early death of Prince Albert in 1861, Queen Victoria's life became tinged with the grey tones of widowhood, and this affected the use of her horses. In a book published in 1874 we find the following passages:

Queen Victoria

'Since the death of the Prince Consort, the State coach and its team of eight gigantic cream stallions has never been used, but the breed is still carefully preserved in the Royal paddocks at Hampton Court.'

The creams were, however, used in the procession during the celebrations in 1887 of the Queen's Golden Jubilee. Her Majesty decided against using the Gold State Coach and chose instead to travel in what she described as *'a handsomely gilt Landau drawn by six of the creams'*, which were driven by postillion riders.

1887 was also the year when Queen Victoria's well-known association with donkeys began. Approaching the age of seventy and experiencing difficulty in walking, she was seeking another method of getting about, and while on a visit to Aix-les-Bains in France she met a peasant driving a donkey and immediately decided to buy it. Known as 'Jacquot', this little donkey became a great pet and went everywhere with Her Majesty, even on trips abroad where, despite the immaculate appearance of her tiny carriage and harness, the sight of the Queen of England driving a donkey caused considerable astonishment.

Although over the next twelve years Queen Victoria continued to describe her horses and carriages – and for her Diamond Jubilee she again refused to use the Gold State Coach in favour of her State Landau, but drawn this time by *eight* cream horses – it was apparent that donkeys were now her favourites. From his photograph 'Jacquot' appears to have been dark-coated, but she also possessed a white donkey and it was

The Landau used both for Queen Victoria's Golden as well as Diamond Jubilee celebrations.

One of the last photographs taken of Queen Victoria, at the reins of a white donkey to a low pony phaeton in 1900. (Reproduced by gracious permission of Her Majesty The Queen)

with this one that she was photographed shortly before her death in 1901 on the Isle of Wight.

Meticulous to the last, Queen Victoria had left instructions regarding her funeral, which, to the surprise of many, she had stipulated was to be a military one. It was for this reason, therefore, that a gun-carriage and not a hearse was used. Another surprise was that after the years of deep mourning following her widowhood, the Queen had requested that her funeral trappings be *white*. The pall covering her coffin was therefore white, draped by a scarlet and purple gold-embroidered cloth on which, on a red velvet cushion, was laid the crown, with orb, sceptre, and insignia of the Garter in front of it.

For the procession through London between Victoria and Paddington stations, the gun-carriage was drawn by her team of eight cream horses in crimson and gilt-encrusted State harness, their manes as usual plaited with purple braid, driven by four postillion riders, accompanied by eight attendants on foot – all wearing scarlet and gold State livery. Behind, and on either side of the gun-carriage, walked a detachment of the Guards, followed by the Household Cavalry in scarlet capes and with nodding plumes in their steel helmets, so that the cortège had an almost festive appearance.

But while the creams had been used in London, it was *not* the blacks, but a team from the Royal Horse Artillery which awaited the Queen's coffin at Windsor Station. These horses, perhaps fractious after a long wait in the cold, jibbed badly on starting and broke some traces, so they were removed, and sailors from the Naval Guard of Honour pulled the gun-carriage on its penultimate journey to St George's Chapel at the Castle.

Two days later, and after some rehearsals, the Royal Artillery team was again put to the gun-carriage, and so it was *by horses* that on Monday, February 4th 1901, Queen Victoria was taken to her final resting place at Frogmore.

King Edward VII

A LTHOUGH King Edward VII's coronation in 1902 did not take place until a full eighteen months after the death of his mother, Queen Victoria, he decided to attend the official Opening of Parliament three weeks later, and to use the Gold State Coach. As, however, this coach had not been out since 1861, it was arranged that it should first be sent to the Royal coachbuilders, Messrs Hooper & Co., for a thorough overhaul and renovation – precisely *seven* days being the time allotted for this undoubtedly time-consuming operation.

Not only did Hooper's achieve this quite remarkable feat, which also included the removal of the box-seat, but, having at the same time been commissioned to build a new State Landau for His Majesty's coronation, they produced a small commemorative booklet containing full details and illustrations of both these carriages, including every stage of the Landau's construction. In this are also printed press reports from *The Times*, *The Morning Post*, *The Daily Telegraph*, as well as from the Paris *Figaro*, all praising the appearance of the newly-furbished Gold coach and the speed with which its renovation was completed, together with compliments on the building of the new State Landau.

The following year, the coronation, originally planned for June, but postponed on account of the King's health to August, took place, and festivities were arranged to span over two days. On the first, King Edward, accompanied by Queen Alexandra, was to travel to and from his coronation in the Gold State Coach, now drawn by postillion-driven horses so that Their Majesties were made more easily visible to the public, while on the second, the new State Landau was to be used.

After having been overhauled and renovated, and with the box-seat removed, in precisely seven days, Messrs Hooper & Co. Ltd proudly included this photograph of King George III's Gold State Coach in the commemorative booklet which they produced in 1902.

This magnificent vehicle, which had been designed by Hooper's managing director, John Robertson, was widely admired when it made its appearance. Its fittings were sumptuous in the extreme: over eighteen feet in length and built on a C-spring under-carriage, its panels were painted in a lighter shade of maroon than the other Royal carriages; and mouldings, carved and gilded in a design of oak leaves, over-lapping each other, outlined its contours. Another, and unusual feature was the splasherboard, which was made of crimson, as opposed to black, patent leather. Japanned, or *patent* leather as it is now known, was a British invention patented (hence its name) at the Great Exhibition in 1851.

Designed to be drawn by postillion-driven horses, this Landau was also fitted with a powerful brake on the hind wheels which, like those in front, were fitted with rubber, instead of iron, tyres. The chief source of pride, however, was the fact that it was almost entirely British made, the only imported items being the pine and mahogany used in the panels; the ash of the body, the elm of the wheelstock, and the oak of the spokes, having been grown in British soil. Similarly, the crimson satin used for the upholstery had been woven in Spitalfields, as were the silken laces; the leather

King Edward VII and Queen Alexandra in the Gold State Coach after his coronation in 1902. It will be noted that the coachman's box-seat has been removed so that Their Majesties could be better seen. Painting by Sidney Paget. (Photo: Illustrated London News)

was tanned and curried (dressed) by Connolly Bros of Euston Road, while the entire vehicle had been built at Hooper's Coachworks in Chelsea.

Hooper's, who were one of several coachbuilders holding the Royal Warrant, had previously converted an ordinary Town Coach, built in 1865, into a Glass State Coach. This alteration was made in 1893, for Queen Alexandra, when she was Princess of Wales, and with its dome-shaped roof, and elegant lines, this attractive little coach was extensively used by both the Princess and her husband when attending evening functions. After King Edward's death in 1910 it was transferred to Marlborough House for Queen Alexandra's exclusive use, until it was eventually returned to the Royal Mews where, known as Queen Alexandra's State Coach, it is still in use today.

Another, larger and less ornate coach, which is also in existence, is King Edward VII's Town Coach. Painted traditionally with a maroon-coloured body, but with a sparsely-trimmed hammercloth in dark blue – as opposed to the more usual scarlet and gold, it was found at Windsor, where it had been stored for many years. It is used mostly for conveying Ambassadors, but Lady Churchill travelled in it at the State funeral according to her husband, Sir Winston Churchill, in 1965.

Building the body (above) and C-spring undercarriage (below) of King Edward II's State Landau in Hooper & Co.'s workshop in 1902. (Photos from a commemorative booklet produced by Hooper & Co.)

Above: The rumble seat and wheels of the State Landau. Below: Described as 'in the wood and iron', the State Landau ready to be painted. (Photos from a commemorative booklet produced by Hooper & Co.)

BUILT BY HOOPER & Co., Ltd.
Designed by John Robertson, *Managing Director*

King Edward VII's magnificent State Landau in all its glory. (Photo from a commemorative booklet produced by Hooper & Co.)

This photograph, described as 'The Glass Coach of the Prince of Wales', appeared in the book produced by the Worshipful Company of Coachmakers and Coach Harnessmakers. It is now known as 'Queen Alexandra's State Coach' and is used, amongst other functions, for carrying the Crown to the State Opening of Parliament, while The Queen travels in the Irish State Coach.

King Edward VII

In addition to official journeys in State coaches and carriages, King Edward and Queen Alexandra both made frequent outings in less exalted vehicles. King Edward, whose enthusiasm for every type of sport was well known, often attended meets of the exclusive Four-in-Hand and Coaching Clubs, for, in May 1872, when he was Prince of Wales, he drove in an ordinary Landau along the banks of the Serpentine to be saluted by members driving their teams in Hyde Park. Four years later, His Royal Highness travelled on the box-seat of the President's coach, when the Four-in-Hand Club drove to the Crystal Palace.

Queen Alexandra too attended these functions. Once, when she was Princess of Wales, she drove to Hyde Park in a Victoria drawn by a fine pair of greys, to see a meet of the Coaching Club attended by no less than twenty-two four-in-hand teams; while on July 3rd 1909, when she was Queen, and accompanied by one of her daughters,

The Prince of Wales (later King Edward VII) arriving at a meet of the Coaching Club, on the box-seat of the President's coach, at Alexandra Palace on 1st July 1876.

61

Members of the Coaching Club saluting the Prince of Wales (later King Edward VII) at a meet held in May 1872 in Hyde Park. The Club founded in 1871, continues to meet on the banks of the Serpentine every year to this day.

Her Royal Highness the Princess Louise, Duchess of Fife, accompanied by her father, the Prince of Wales, driving a pony to a ralli-car, in about 1890. (Reproduced by gracious permission of Her Majesty The Queen)

she was photographed on her way to the Club's eighty-second meet, with a very smart pair of chestnuts driven to her Victoria.

When in London, Queen Alexandra was always driven by a coachman with a liveried groom in attendance, but whilst at home in Sandringham she preferred to drive herself. On account of this pastime, as well as to compensate for her disappointment at not being allowed to accompany her husband on his tour of India, he gave her in 1875 an enchanting little cane-bodied phaeton built by Belvalette Frères in Paris. Today this is still a favourite vehicle with the Royal Family.

With this little phaeton it was possible to drive either a single pony or a pair of ponies, but it was not long before this intrepid Royal 'whip' had progressed to the driving of a tandem. In 1888, and to celebrate the Royal couple's silver wedding anniversary, the *Illustrated London News* published an engraving of the Princess of Wales at the reins of a tandem of ponies to a dog-cart, surrounded by her family.

Queen Alexandra's driving was, however, a source of fright to several people, amongst them her daughter-in-law, the Princess May, who reported being terrified when driven at speed in the grounds of Sandringham. Another contemporary writer also described a hair-raising journey by tandem, when a corner was turned so sharply that the vehicle tilted dangerously onto one wheel.

Not unexpectedly, the five children of King Edward VII and Queen Alexandra were also keen 'whips', both Prince Eddy and Prince George (later King George V) having been reported as driving. Among the Royal Archives are photographs of the Princess Louise (later Duchess of Fife) accompanied by her father, at the reins of a pony to a ralli-car, while another depicts the Princesses Maud (who became Queen of Norway) and Victoria with a smaller turnout drawn by a donkey.

At this time, vehicles were often presented to members of the Royal Family, and amongst some unusual ones were a South African Cape Cart and a Hansom Cab. The latter was given to the Prince of Wales in November 1872 after a display of London Cabs (both two- and four-wheeled) had taken place at Marlborough House. This was staged to encourage improvements in cabs, with prizes from the Royal Society of Arts, and the Prince, as the Society's President, inspected all the vehicles, finally expressing the wish to have a Hansom Cab *'for use at Sandringham'*.

At the beginning of King Edward's reign there had been an upsurge in coachbuilding, when, after years of some austerity caused by Queen Victoria's widowhood, many of the Peers attending his coronation ordered new State coaches and chariots. The weekly parades of carriages in Hyde Park on Sunday mornings were also indicative of an era of wealth and opulence, but towards the end of his reign, the new threat to horse-transport, the motorcar, had arrived, and this started a gradual decline in the use of carriages.

When King Edward died, it was decided not to risk the possibility of another fracas with horses such as had occurred nine years previously at the funeral of his mother,

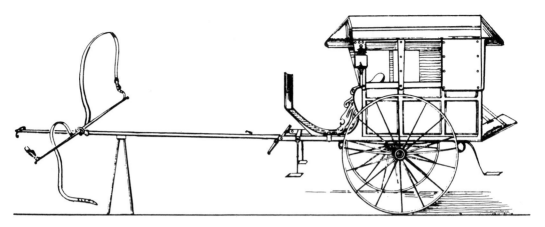

The Cape Cart which Prince Albert Victor and his younger brother, Prince George (who later became King George V), brought back from South Africa as a present for their parents, the Prince and Princess of Wales.

Her Majesty Queen Alexandra, accompanied by the Princess Victoria, driving in a Victoria, at the 82nd meet of the Four-in-Hand Club held in Hyde Park on 3rd July 1909. Queen Alexandra, being a keen driver of horses, often attended functions of this sort.

Two of Queen Victoria's cream Hanoverian stallions in State harness, in the Royal Mews. From a painting by Lutyens, 1884. (Photo by kind permission of His Grace the Duke of Westminster, DL)

King George V and Queen Mary returning from Ascot. This painting, which at present hangs in the Royal Mews, is one of two commissioned by Queen Mary, by Sir Alfred Munnings. (Reproduced by permission of the Tate Gallery)

Held by Head Coachman Arthur Showell, and with their manes plaited intricately with silver braid, the team of four Windsor greys awaits the newly married Prince and Princess of Wales in 1981. (Photo by kind permission of Judy Appelbee)

After their wedding in 1986, the Duke and Duchess of York in the State Landau built for King Edward VII in 1902 by Hooper & Co. (Photo: Alpha)

On the occasion of their Silver Wedding anniversary in 1888, the Prince and Princess of Wales (later King Edward VII and Queen Alexandra), posed for this picture, surrounded by their family, at Sandringham. Queen Alexandra was a noted driver of a tandem, and this picture demonstrates the correct method for a groom to hold the reins of both horses when driven in this fashion. (Photo: Illustrated London News)

Queen Victoria. The Navy was therefore asked to provide man-power for the pulling of a gun-carriage at Windsor, and it has been traditional for sailors to perform this function at Royal funerals ever since.

For the procession in London, however, the Royal Horse Artillery again produced a team, and King Edward, who was always regarded as an arbiter of fashion, fun and sport, might perhaps have enjoyed knowing that his funeral in 1910 made history in that he was the last British monarch to have had the gun-carriage containing his coffin drawn by horses.

✑ *King George V* ✑

KING GEORGE V was the very last monarch to have attended his coronation in the Gold State Coach drawn by a team of cream-coloured horses. These had been kept for the Sovereign's exclusive use ever since their introduction into England in 1714, afterwards being bred at Hampton Court, but, due to the difficulty of obtaining fresh blood, and consequent in-breeding, they gradually died out. King George, however, may well not have regretted their decline, since in a letter to his mother describing his first Opening of Parliament ceremony, he complained of the Creams being '*rather unruly*' and that '*the leaders shied right across the street every time they came to a band .*'

His Majesty's reference to the Gold State Coach was merely that it was '*not uncomfortable, but very high*', and four months later, on June 22nd 1911, when he travelled in it again, this time to his coronation, there were no adverse comments about the behaviour of the horses, just a description from Queen Mary that '*the cream horses looked so pretty, with a touch of lavender blue decorating their manes.*'

For this coronation, one new carriage was purchased. This was the Glass Coach, so named on account of its having larger windows than were usual at that time. It had originally been built as a Sheriff's Town coach by Peters & Son. Later in George V's reign, a near-tragedy occurred when the Irish State Coach was at the coachbuilding firm of Barker & Co. and a fire at their premises destroyed all its woodwork. The ornate metal portions were, however, saved, and so, by means of photographs, Messrs Barker were able to reconstruct the entire vehicle, at the same time proudly producing an elaborately drawn leaflet depicting the coach, which stated that in February 1912, they had *built*, not *re*built it.

Apart from the Royal carriages, King George and Queen Mary were the owners of at least two other vehicles, both given to them in 1893 as wedding presents. One was from the Sandringham Estate workers, while the other, a Wagonette, was the gift of Lord Lonsdale, the famous 'Yellow Earl'. This latter was unusual in that it had two hoods to cover the seats at the rear; it became known as the 'Lonsdale Wagonette'.

Both King George and Queen Mary enjoyed driving. Before his marriage, and when as Prince George he was serving as a Naval officer in Malta, the King was reported

King George V and Queen Mary in the Gold State coach drawn by a team of eight cream horses – the very last time they were to be used for a coronation procession. (Photo: Illustrated London News)

as having driven his three young cousins in a high two-wheeled dog-cart, with 'Cocky', his brown cob.

Queen Mary, when she was Princess May, was also the recipient of a vehicle, for when she lived with her parents at White Lodge in Richmond Park, the neighbouring tradesmen gave her a complete turnout as a twenty-first birthday present. This consisted of an elegant lady's phaeton with a pony, harness, and two rugs – a bear-skin for winter, and a light one with her monogram on for summer – as well as two whips, one of which had a parasol attached. The Princess is recorded as having been '*so pleased and delighted*' with this gift, which was a smaller edition of the one used by her mother.

At their home, her parents, the Duke and Duchess of Teck, kept the following vehicles: a Barouche, a Landau, a Wagonette, and a dog-cart, together with four carriage horses, the phaeton horse 'Jumbo', and one other. Their head coachman, Kitchener, had two under-coachmen in addition to grooms, and he was reputed as having been able to drive to London – a distance of about eight miles – in record time, helped

Queen Mary, when she was Princess May of Teck, at the reins of the horse which together with the phaeton, harness, rug, and whip, were presented to her by the inhabitants of Richmond, Surrey, on the occasion of her twenty-first birthday. This photograph was taken outside White Lodge in Richmond Park, where she was then living with her parents, the Duke and Duchess of Teck. (Reproduced by gracious permission of Her Majesty The Queen)

The coach which belonged to Queen Mary's mother, the Duchess of Teck. This photograph appeared in the book produced by the Worshipful Company of Coachmakers and Coach Harnessmakers.

of course by the police who, when they saw him coming, always cleared the way.

White Lodge, a beautiful Georgian house situated on rising ground in Richmond Park, was an ideal place from which to drive for pleasure, and there are several accounts of the Princess May's outings there with her cousin, the Princess Alice, and the Princess Louise, Duchess of Fife, who lived just outside the Park, at Sheen Lodge. Princess May did not, however, confine her driving to Richmond Park, for the contemporary magazine *The Road* reported that in 1892 the Princess had '*insisted upon following the Royal party to watch the tennis at Wimbledon by driving her own little pony trap*', and she was also described as being a '*first-class whip*'.

Privacy, when indulging in private pursuits, has understandably always been the wish of Royalty, and in 1891, when Princess May was engaged to the Duke of Clarence (Prince Eddy), the elder son of the Prince and Princess of Wales, she and her fiancé were delighted at managing to remain incognito when out driving in London in his father's Hansom Cab. But their happiness was sadly short-lived. Prince Eddy contracted influenza, which turned swiftly to pneumonia, and on January 14th 1892, almost a month before the date fixed for their wedding, he died.

History does not, however, come to a halt with tragedy, and the grief experienced by both the Princess May and by Prince Eddy's brother, George, inevitably drew them together. It is heartening therefore to read that after being taken down to Eastbourne to recover from the shock of her fiancé's death, Princess May was out driving in a Wagonette along the Downs, accompanied by her cousins, and that a year later, she and Prince George had become engaged.

The wedding of Princess May to Prince George – who had now been given the title of Duke of York – took place on July 6th, 1893. The day was both hot and sunny, and therefore possible for the twelve Landaus transporting guests to the ceremony in the first procession to have their hoods down. Queen Victoria, however, travelled in a closed carriage – for once being stumped by its correct nomenclature and describing it as '*a sort of State Coach, with many windows*'. In fact, it may have been the pretty little coach now known as 'Queen Alexandra's Coach', which had that year been fitted with new, and more, glass windows.

After their marriage, the new Duke and Duchess of York departed for Sandringham to spend their honeymoon in York Cottage. This was also to remain their country home for the next thirty-three years and they immediately built stables to house sixteen horses. Later, when the Duchess of Teck visited her daughter and son-in-law, she complained that York Cottage was much too small, while the stables were far too big – a rather similar situation to that of the Prince Regent when he was building his Pavilion at Brighton.

Within a few years the Duke and Duchess of York were proud parents, and nursery photographs depict both Prince Edward (who was to become the uncrowned King Edward VIII) 'driving' a toy wooden horse, and his brother (who succeeded him as

Above: Prince Albert of York, who became King George VI, in his 'Galloper' – a type of baby carriage in which a pair of toy horses moved alternately on either side of the single front wheel. (Reproduced by gracious permission of Her Majesty The Queen)

Opposite: At the reins of a favourite toy pony and cart, the Prince Edward (who later became King Edward VIII and then Duke of Windsor) accompanied by his little brother, the Prince Albert, who was later King George VI. (Reproduced by gracious permission of Her Majesty The Queen)

King George VI) sitting in a fascinating type of baby-carriage called a 'Galloper'. This had a pair of toy horses attached to a central front wheel, the horses moving up and down when the pram was pushed from behind; it was a very favourite vehicle of Edwardian children. Another photograph of the Royal brothers, accompanied this time by their sister, Princess Mary, shows her at the reins of a Shetland pony, with a most elegant little phaeton. On account of their interest in driving, in 1905 the Showmen of England presented the Royal children with an exquisite little pony-sized Landau, and this is still among the collection of miniature carriages in the Royal Mews.

Throughout their lives, Queen Mary and her mother kept notes of daily events, either in letters or in their diaries. Thus we learn how Princess Augusta, Duchess of Cambridge (Queen Mary's grandmother), narrowly escaped injury in an accident on the Kew Road when her Brougham was overturned by a Hansom Cab. And in 1886 Princess May reported: '*Mama and Sir Thomas [Lander] drove in the pony carriage, Sir H[ubert Miller] and I in the tandem . . .*' – although who was at the reins of the tandem

This enchanting miniature Landau, seen here drawn by a pair of the recently discovered breed of Caspian ponies, was presented to the children of King George V and Queen Mary in 1905 by the Showmen of England. (Reproduced by gracious permission of Her Majesty The Queen)

is not quite clear. Also, during this year, and when she was a visitor to Sandringham, Princess May recorded an outing with four Hungarian horses driven by a Hungarian, adding: '*we did go it fast!*' and a varnished Hungarian phaeton remains in the Royal collection of carriages. Nor, as an experienced 'whip' herself, did Princess May ever get over her fright at being driven by Queen Alexandra!

Precisely three years after King George V's accession to the throne, the First World War broke out, and while this did not restrict *all* horse transport, its decline became more rapid due to the fact that many horses were commandeered for use by the Army, and also because motorised vehicles were on the increase. It is therefore not until four years later, when peace had been declared, that there are accounts of King George and Queen Mary using carriages.

By 1920, the cream horses had finally died out and been replaced with greys – which, not being a particular breed, were less likely to become temperamental and were more easily obtained. Previously, small grey horses – almost ponies – had been used at Wind-

Standing beside the Shetland pony, the Prince Edward (later King Edward VIII and Duke of Windsor) with, in the miniature phaeton, his sister, the Princess Mary, and brother, the Prince Albert (later King George VI). (Reproduced by gracious permission of Her Majesty The Queen)

Their Majesties King George V and Queen Mary driving through Windsor Great Park to Ascot races. This is one of two paintings by Sir Alfred Munnings commissioned by Queen Mary. (Reproduced by permission of the Royal Academy of Arts)

sor for drawing lighter carriages, but for heavy vehicles, such as the Gold State Coach, larger horses were required. On account of the fact that greys had originally been used at Windsor, and that the King had decided to change his family's name from Saxe-Coburg and Gotha to that of Windsor, the greys received the attractive-sounding title of 'Windsor greys', by which name they have been known ever since.

Although there were also Cleveland Bay horses in the Royal Mews, from this date on, the greys were much in evidence, and many photographs were taken of the King and Queen driving in carriages drawn by these horses upon ceremonial and other occasions. Proof, however, that Queen Mary was proud of the Windsor greys lies in the fact that in 1925 she commissioned Sir Alfred Munnings to paint two pictures of them. One depicts Their Majesties returning from Ascot in a Landau drawn by a postillion-driven team of four greys, while the other shows the entire procession of Landaus with both greys and bay horses, in Windsor Great Park.

In May 1935, King George V celebrated twenty-five years on the throne with a drive through London to a service of thanksgiving at St Paul's Cathedral, and, as was usual, he and Queen Mary were accorded a tumultuous reception by the crowds lining the streets. On this occasion, however, it so impressed His Majesty that shortly before his last illness he is recorded to have said: '*I had no idea that I was so popular. I am beginning to think they must really like me for myself.*' When he died a few months later, he did so secure in the knowledge that he had been both *loved* and liked.

King George VI

THE SADLY all-too short reign of King George VI was largely marred by the Second World War, leaving little room for carriage pageantry. War broke out two years after his coronation and lasted for six out of his fifteen years on the throne. This coronation procession was, however, notable in that for the very first time grey horses were used to draw the Gold State Coach. Despite the fact that His Majesty is quoted as having described the journey in this coach as one of the most uncomfortable he had ever made, he again travelled in it for the State Opening of Parliament the following year.

During the war, when on holiday with his family at Sandringham, the King, accompanied by his two young daughters, used to ride round the estate either on horseback or by bicycle, while the Queen, following the tradition set by both Queen Alexandra and Queen Mary, took to driving a pony in a Governess Car. This is depicted in a particularly happy photograph.

At an early age, the two little Princesses learned to drive their ponies, and Princess Margaret, accompanied by her sister, drove an attractive little pony named 'Snowball' to a spindle-sided Governess Car, in the grounds of Windsor Castle. A few years later, both Princesses competed in the show-ring, for it is recorded that in 1944, Princess Margaret won the Utility Class at Royal Windsor Horse Show with a Fell pony to a Governess Car. The following year it was the future Queen's turn, when, as Princess Elizabeth, she won the Open Class at this same show, also driving the Fell pony, but this time to Queen Alexandra's favourite little cane-bodied French chaise.

This little chaise was always a popular vehicle with the Royal family, for another happy photograph shows the then Princess Elizabeth, accompanied this time by her

Queen Elizabeth (now the Queen Mother) accompanied by a groom, with her husband, King George VI, and their two daughters on bicycles in the grounds of Sandringham during the war. The Governess Car which Her Majesty is driving is interesting in that it has a circular high front panel in the dash-board – which was built in so that ladies could not see their horses' posteriors. (Photo: The Times*)*

Opposite: King George VI and Queen Elizabeth in the Gold State Coach on their way to his coronation in 1937. (Photo: Illustrated London News*)*

Their Majesties King George VI and Queen Elizabeth driving round the White City Stadium in a barouche, prior to the men's show-jumping class for the King George V Gold Cup at the Royal International Horse Show in 1950. (Photo: Keystone Press Agency)

mother, the Queen, setting out for a drive in Windsor Great Park, with yet another pony.

With the cessation of war in 1945, things began returning to normal within the Royal Mews, and carriages were again used on official occasions. In 1950, the King, accompanied by his Queen, made history at the Royal International Horse Show by arriving with his retinue in open barouches and driving round the track of the White City Stadium. This was prior to his presenting the Gold Cup, given by his father, King George V, for a men's show-jumping class.

By this time, however, it was apparent to everyone that His Majesty was seriously ill, yet he continued to make every effort to attend to all his many duties. It was therefore a great shock to the nation, and indeed to the whole world, from whom he had gained genuine affection, when on February 6th 1952, it was learned that the King had passed away in his sleep overnight, a quiet, gentle, and conscientious monarch to the end.

Watched by the Duchess of Kent, King George VI and Queen Elizabeth, and the Duke of Beaufort, The Queen, when she was Princess Elizabeth, driving a Fell pony to the French chaise at Royal Windsor Horse Show in 1945. (Photo: Photo News Agency)

Her Royal Highness the Princess Margaret, accompanied by her sister, the Princess Elizabeth (now Her Majesty The Queen) driving 'Snowball' to a spindle-sided Governess Car at Windsor.

Queen Elizabeth II

IN 1952, and although the British nation was mourning the loss of its much-loved monarch, King George VI, the coronation of his daughter was, after years of wartime austerity, looked forward to keenly. When it also became known that on account of the young Queen's great love of horses, carriages were to form a large part of the procession, excitement not only mounted, but the search for more harness horses became a priority.

At that time there was still a number of light trade horses in use in London, as well as a surprising, although small revival in the driving of four-in-hands, so several directors of commercial firms, together with members of the Coaching Club were invited to lend their horses to be driven as pairs, and to take part as coachmen themselves. With this extra help, most of the foreign Heads of States and Prime Ministers attending the coronation were driven to it in carriages.

Within the Royal Mews, there was of course a number of vehicles for use on official occasions. These comprised the Irish State Coach, Queen Alexandra's State Coach, the Glass Coach, State Landaus, Barouches, Clarences and Broughams, and all had been kept in immaculate condition, but the oldest and most valuable carriage, the Gold State Coach, which had been built in 1761 for King George III, and in which by tradition, The Queen would travel to and from her coronation, was the one to cause most problems.

As a precaution against damage by enemy action, this coach had been stored throughout the war years at Mentmore in Bedfordshire (then the home of the late Lord Rosebery). Unfortunately it was found to have developed dry rot in the door panels. To renew the woodwork of any other vehicle would not have been too difficult, but since the body of the Gold Coach was decorated with valuable paintings by the eighteenth-century Italian artist, Cipriani, it appeared at first to be an almost insurmountable task.

A brilliant idea was, however, evolved by means of which the precious paintings were covered with layers of paper, pasted on until they formed a stiff outer 'skin'. The offending wood behind was carefully whittled away with a surgeon's scalpel until only the rear of the paintings was visible. These were then transposed onto a fine

The Windsor greys in State harness being put to the Gold State Coach for the coronation of Her Majesty The Queen in 1953. A painting by the late Mr Lionel Edwards.

silk backing before being eased on to new wooden panels and secured with adhesive. Finally, the laborious and nerve-racking task of soaking off the layers of paper eventually revealed Cipriani's paintings complete and undamaged.

In addition to the bodywork being thoroughly overhauled, the interior of the Gold Coach was re-upholstered and fitted with new, and more comfortable foam-rubber cushions covered with crimson velvet. One completely modern innovation was the fitting of battery-operated electric lights under the roof. It was feared that if coronation day were bright and sunny then the interior of the coach would be too dark for the Press to obtain good photographs of The Queen. But it was then realised that this new lighting might interfere with television reception, so 'suppressors' had to be installed – a problem which had of course never been envisaged in any previous coronations.

Although June 2nd 1953 proved to be a day which was dull, wet and extremely cold, the sight of the newly furbished Gold State Coach was even more spectacular

Framed by a window of the Irish State Coach, Her Majesty The Queen driving to the State Opening of Parliament after her coronation in 1953. This photograph rightly won an award as being one of the best and most popular ones taken.

than expected. Its team of eight grey horses wore ornate State harness made from maroon-coloured Morocco leather embellished with gilt fittings, and were driven by four postillion riders wearing scarlet jackets trimmed with gold braid. Within the coach, and under pearl-tinted lighting, the sight of the radiant young Queen, sparkling with diamonds, Prince Philip in Naval uniform beside her, was breathtaking.

So, to the clicking and whirring of cameras, and amid echoing cheers from the crowds lining the route, the new monarch, Elizabeth II, made her first appearance as Queen of the United Kingdom.

Her Majesty The Queen and the Duke of Edinburgh in a State Landau after the ceremony of touching the sword at the City of London boundary on 12th June, 1953. (Photo: Sport & General Agency)

In the driving world, Her Majesty's coronation had far-reaching effects. Suddenly, harness horses, carriages, and driving accoutrements were in demand, and the following year at the Royal Agricultural Society's annual show, held that year at Windsor Great Park, a pageant and parade of carriages was put on, with twelve of the sixty on view having been lent from the Royal Mews. These ranged from the Ascot Landau, which was built for Queen Victoria; the Royal State Dress Landau; the Royal State Barouche; Queen Victoria's Ivory-mounted Phaeton; the char-à-banc presented in 1844 to the Queen by King Louis-Philippe of France, down to five miniature vehicles drawn by

Her Majesty The Queen driving a pony to a phaeton in India whilst on a State visit in 1961. (Photo: Planet News Ltd)

ponies. Everyone able to do so, produced and drove their horses and ponies, and it was at this show that the idea of forming the now successful British Driving Society was mooted.

As has been already recorded, during their early years, both The Queen and her sister, the Princess Margaret, drove their ponies, and although when she grew older, Her Majesty's preference veered more towards riding, she has in fact also been seen driving. On a State visit to India in 1961, she was photographed driving a native pony, while later, and at Windsor, when Prince Andrew was a toddler, she took him for a drive in Queen Alexandra's beautiful little cane-bodied phaeton, drawn by a pair of New Forest ponies.

HRH The Princess Anne driving a pair of Haflinger ponies to a French chaise when she became the 1000th member of the British Driving Society in 1969. (Photo: Keystone Press Agency)

Royal children become accustomed from infancy to travelling in horse-drawn vehicles, and continuing his family's association with equine toys, Prince Charles, as a little boy, appears to have enjoyed playing with an enchanting miniature gig and and pony made from varnished wood – in which he was photographed with the reins in his hands. Later, as an adult and having become Prince of Wales, he thrilled members of the British Driving Society when, in 1976, he not only joined it, but also drove a smart pair of greys to a Demi-Mail Phaeton in the Concours d'Elegance class held at its annual show on Smith's Lawn at Windsor.

Princess Anne, too, began to drive when she first grew up, for in 1969, after The Queen had been presented with a pair of Haflinger ponies, Her Royal Highness, accom-

Prince Charles aged two in his toy gig and pony. (Photo : John Scott, courtesy of Mrs Appelbee)

panied by her little brother, the Prince Edward, drove them to the cane-bodied French chaise at both the Royal Windsor Horse Show, and at the annual show organised by the British Driving Society, which she had graciously agreed to join as its 1000th member.

The horse world has always felt honoured by the amount of interest shown by The Queen and her family in every branch of equine sport, but it was not until 1971 that driving began to play a part within the Royal household. This started when the Duke of Edinburgh decided to retire from playing polo, and honoured the Coaching Club by attending its centenary meet and dinner. Here, His Royal Highness was presented with a leather-bound copy of a book on the art of driving, and in his speech, jokingly said that he would '*take the hint*'.

A perfectionist in all he does, it was not long after having started with a pair of horses that the Duke was handling a four-in-hand with considerable skill. It was he, too, who as President of the Federation Equestre Internationale, first introduced into Britain the exciting sport of three-day event driving, which he had seen being performed on the Continent and in which he decided also to take part.

The first international driving competition to be held in this country took place in 1971 at the Royal Windsor Horse Show, where they have been staged annually ever since. Similar trials for European and World Championships are held in different countries on alternate years.

With Prince Philip's enthusiastic encouragement, a British team comprising three four-in-hand drivers was sent to the first World Driving Championships held in Germany in 1972, where they won the coveted gold medal. After that, His Royal Highness was selected as a member of the British team for several events, and thereby helped to win two bronze medals and yet another gold, while in 1982, he succeeded in winning the Individual Championship at the international competition held at Royal Windsor Horse Show.

In addition to these successes, the Duke has produced for posterity the very first book to be written on the subject of competition driving. In this he has recorded not only a great deal of informative and technical detail, but also, and with a lively wit, his own personal experiences – some quite hair-raising – which makes it of appeal to spectators as well as to competitors in the sport.

Prince Philip's participation in driving has also caused a revival in the many different trades associated with it – the construction of new carriages being perhaps the most impressive, since a great deal of long-forgotten craftsmanship is involved. Modern

HRH The Prince of Wales driving a Demi-Mail Phaeton at the British Driving Society's Show at Windsor in 1976, when he won a runner-up award in the Concours d'Elegance, and joined the Society as its 2000th member. (Photo: The Times)

HRH The Duke of Edinburgh driving a team of Cleveland Bay/Thoroughbred horses at one of the first driving events held at Lowther Castle in 1973. (Photo: Findlay Davidson)

A drawing of a modern vehicle built by Michael Mart for use by HRH The Duke of Edinburgh for driving events.

HRH The Duke of Edinburgh leading foreign competitors up the Long Walk at Windsor during the World Driving Championships held at Windsor in 1980.

89

HRH The Duke of Edinburgh driving Her Majesty The Queen in a dog-cart with a pair of Fell ponies, when members of the British Driving Society presented Her Majesty with loyal greetings at Balmoral during the Silver Jubilee celebrations in 1977. (Photo: Aberdeen Journals Ltd)

technology, in the form of plastics, laminated woods, and ball-bearings within wheels, has been introduced, and His Royal Highness has given much constructive advice, particularly with regard to the building of vehicles for his own use in driving events. As a result, a new export trade has been established.

Despite his extremely busy life, Prince Philip has always managed to take an active interest in other people, and so, having consented to become Patron of the British Driving Society in 1973, and realising the degree of fun there was to be had with driving, he immediately wondered whether similar enjoyment could be provided for disabled people. From this suggestion has sprung many 'Driving for the Disabled' groups, some of whom have purchased specially-designed vehicles which enable the transit of wheelchairs. Both the Prince of Wales, and his sister, the Princess Anne, have expressed interest in this latest form of therapy and have attended disabled driving events. Without doubt these have helped to create a new concept of life for very many disabled people.

Throughout the centuries, many foreign breeds of harness horses have been introduced into the Royal Mews, from the original Hanoverian horses imported in Georgian times, to the all-black Dutch Friesians during the reign of Queen Victoria. Although at the present time there are horses from Denmark, Germany, Holland, and Sweden, The Queen has made sure that the original British breed of carriage horse – the Cleveland Bay – remains, and some years ago she purchased the well-known stallion 'Mulgrave Supreme' in order to maintain the future of the breed in this country.

In addition to Her Majesty's stable of bay and grey carriage horses, there are a small number of ponies, for Prince Philip also inaugurated inter-breed obstacle driving competitions, in which he has himself occasionally taken part by driving pairs of golden-coated Haflingers, as well as the black Fell ponies kept at Balmoral. Another, recently introduced breed of pony – the tiny Caspian from Iran – has been put to some of the miniature carriages in the Royal Mews.

Despite the fact that motorcars are more speedy and convenient, The Queen clearly believes in preserving old-time pageantry, realising that she can best be seen in a horse-drawn carriage. For official occasions in Scotland, she therefore uses the Scottish State Coach. This was originally built in 1830 and belonged to the late Queen Mary's mother, the Duchess of Teck. It has now been entirely re-modelled with more and larger windows, and with glass panels in the roof. When in London, the ornate Irish State Coach is used for functions such as the State Opening of Parliament, while, when welcoming foreign dignitaries, and weather permitting, Her Majesty drives in the large State Landau which was built for King Edward VII at the time of his coronation. Another, most picturesque event takes place every year at Royal Ascot, when The Queen and her guests drive down the course in open Landaus in the time-honoured tradition begun by King George IV.

At functions such as Royal weddings, as many carriages as possible are used. This adds to the 'fairy-tale' aura of these occasions, and the sight of Royal brides travelling in the Glass Coach – one of the more modern vehicles, as it was built in 1910 – is memorable. For the last two Royal weddings – those of the Prince of Wales and his brother, the Prince Andrew, both bridegrooms were conveyed to the ceremonies in King Edward VII's massive State Landau, and this carriage provided a perfect setting for the Royal couples' journey back to Buckingham Palace.

All the carriages owned by The Queen are on view to the public, the largest collection being housed in the Royal Mews at Buckingham Palace where the carriage horses are also stabled. The Mews is open every Wednesday and Thursday afternoon throughout the year (unless of course there happens to be a State function taking place on those days). Other, although smaller displays of vehicles are to be found in the Royal Mews at Windsor Castle, and within the Orangery at Hampton Court, where there are also

Royal Cavalcade

The scene outside St Paul's Cathedral after the marriage of the Prince and Princess of Wales in 1981. The Landau used was the one built by Hoopers in 1902 for King Edward VII. (Photo: Courtesy M. Goddard and Sunday Telegraph Magazine)

many other items of historical interest.

In 1977, the nation rejoiced when it celebrated the twenty-fifth year of The Queen's reign. As usually happens on these occasions, commemorative souvenirs of every description were manufactured, including models of the Gold State Coach, but one of the most impressive items ever to have been produced was a full-scale replica of this vehicle which, early in the year, was put on display at the *Daily Mail* Ideal Homes Exhibition at Olympia in London. Made entirely of fibre-glass, and complete with a team of eight life-sized horses in State harness, four postillion riders and accompanying attendants on foot, this mammoth exhibit occupied the length of the main hall, so was easily visible at close quarters by many thousands of visitors before they saw the actual Jubilee procession.

The celebration of The Queen's Silver Jubilee took place on June 7th, and for this historic event the Gold State Coach was again overhauled and re-gilded, while to high-

Her Majesty The Queen, accompanied by the Duke of Edinburgh, in the Gold State Coach on Jubilee Day in 1977. Note the little nosegay of sweetly-scented flowers hanging inside the door, placed there by members of the staff in the Royal Mews. (Photo: Central Press Photos Ltd)

light the occasion, the horses' manes were plaited intricately with silver braid. The Queen herself wore an outfit in pale fondant pink, the colour which both she and the Princess Margaret had worn when, in 1935, and as little girls, they had attended a similar ceremony at St Paul's Cathedral, during the twenty-fifth year of the reign of their grandfather, King George V.

When the Queen appeared in the Gold State Coach, looking as radiant as she had in 1953, it was noticed that hanging inside both doors were tiny nosegays of orange-blossom, lily-of-the-valley and other sweetly scented flowers. These had been supplied as a gesture of loyal affection by the staff in the Royal Mews, and were but a token of the vast quantities of flowers to be showered upon Her Majesty that day, as they have been on all previous and successive occasions. All symbolise the wish:

LONG MAY SHE REIGN.

Bibliography

AIRLIE, Mabell Countess of, *Thatched with Gold*, Hutchinson, 1962.

BATTISCOMBE, Georgina, *Queen Alexandra*, Constable, 1969.

BAXTER BROWN, Michael, *Richmond Park*, Robert Hale, 1985.

BLAND, Olivia, *The Royal Way of Death*, Constable, 1986.

BEAUFORT, 8th Duke of, *Badminton Book of Driving* 1889.

BURNEY, Fanny, *The Diary of Fanny Burney*, J.M. Dent, 1940.

CAMPBELL, Judith, *Royalty on Horseback*, Sidgwick & Jackson, 1974.

CREEVEY, Thomas, *The Creevey Papers*, B.T. Batsford, 1963.

DELDERFIELD, E.R., *Kings & Queens of England*, David & Charles, 1970.

DUFF, David, *Victoria Travels*, F. Muller, 1970.

GARRETT, Richard, *Royal Travel*, Blandford, 1982.

GILBEY, Sir Walter, Bt., *Early Carriages & Roads*, Vinton & Co., 1903.

GILBEY, Sir Walter, Bt., *Modern Carriages*, Vinton & Co., 1905.

GORDON, W.J., *The Horse World of London*, 1893, re-issued J.A. Allen 1971.

KEAY, Douglas, *Queen Elizabeth the Queen Mother*, I.P.C., 1980.

LARWOOD, Jacob, *The Story of the London Parks*, Hotten, 1872.

LONGFORD, Elizabeth Countess of, *Victoria R.I.*, Weidenfeld, 1964.

LONGFORD, Elizabeth Countess of, *The Royal House of Windsor*, Weidenfeld, 1974.

MARIE-LOUISE, H.H. PRINCESS, *My Memories of Six Reigns*, Evans, 1956.

MIDDLEMAS, Keith, *Edward VII*, Weidenfeld, 1972.

MIDDLEMAS, Keith, *George VI*, Weidenfeld, 1974.

MILLER, Sir John, K.C.V.O., D.S.O., M.C., *The Royal Mews*, Pitkin, 1968.

'One of Her Majesty's Servants', *The Private Life of the Queen*, 1897.

PALMER, Alan, *George IV*, Weidenfeld, 1972.

PLOWDEN, Alison, *The Young Victoria*, Weidenfeld, 1981.

POPE-HENNESSEY, James, *Queen Mary*, Allen & Unwin, 1959.

PRIESTLEY, James, *The Prince of Pleasure*, Heinemann, 1967.

REESE, M.M., *Master of the Horse*, Threshold Books, 1976.

SELWAY, N.C., *The Golden Age of Coaching & Sport*, F. Lewis, 1972.

SHONE, A.B., *A Century and a Half of Amateur Driving*, J.A. Allen, 1955.

SIDNEY, S., *The Book of the Horse*, Cassell, 1874.

SITWELL, O., & Barton, M., *Brighton*, Faber, 1935.

THRUPP, G.A., *A History of Coaches*, 1877.

WOODFORDE, the Rev. James, *The Diary of a Country Parson*, Oxford, 1949.

Index

Adelaide, Queen, 39, 46
Albert, Prince Consort, 43–50, 53
Alexandra, Queen, 9, 55–65, 75
Amelia, the Princess, 22
Andrew, the Prince, 84, 91
Andrews, Richard (coachbuilder), 49
Anne, the Princess Royal, 85, 90
Anne, Queen, 20, 21, 23
Arabian horses, 21
Ascot, Royal, 20, 36–7, 74, 91

Balmoral, 90, 91
Barker & Co. (coachbuilders), 43, 66
Barouches (carriages), 9, 39, 42, 46, 47, 67,
    80
Barrymore, Lord, 33
Belvalette Freres (coachbuilders), 63
Bianconi, 47
British Driving Society, 84, 85, 87, 88, 90
Brougham, Lord, 10, 37
Broughams (carriages), 9, 10, 72, 80
Buckingham, House/Palace, 27, 36, 39, 91
Burney, Fanny, 26, 39

Cape Cart (South African vehicle), 63
Carlton House, 28, 31
Caspian ponies, 72, 91
Chaise (carriage), 8
Chambers, Sir William, 23
Char-à-banc (carriage), 44, 83
Charles I, King, 15, 16, 19
Charles II, King, 17–19, 20
Charles, Prince of Wales, 9, 85–7, 90, 92
Charlotte, Princess, 34
Charlotte, Queen, 26
Cipriani (artist), 24, 80, 81
Clarence (carriage), 10, 80

Cleveland Bay (horse), 51, 74, 88, 91
Coaching Club, 61, 62, 80
Coachmakers, The Worshipful Company of,
    8, 18, 60, 68
Cook, William (coachbuilder), 29, 30, 31
Connolly Bros. (curriers), 57
Corben, of Twickenham (coachbuilder), 39,
    46
Cromwell, Oliver, 16, 17, 28
Curricle (carriage), 31

Dog-carts (carriages), 9, 67
Driving for the Disabled, 90

Edward VII, King, 9, 23, 45, 46, 55–65, 91
Edward VIII, Duke of Windsor, 69–73
Edward, the Prince, 86
Elizabeth I, 8, 11–14
Elizabeth II, HM The Queen, 9, 75, 77, 79,
    80–93
Elizabeth, HM The Queen Mother, 75–9
Exhibition, the Great, 8, 47–9, 56

Fell ponies, 75, 79, 90, 91
Felton, William (coachbuilder), 10
Forgon (carriage), 24
Friesian horses, 19, 52, 91

Gautier et Picheron (coachbuilders), 44
Gelderlander horses, 19
George I, King, 14, 21, 22
George II, King, 22, 23
George III, King, 8, 9, 23–7
George IV, King, 8, 28–37, 40, 91
George V, King, 9, 66–75, 78, 93
George VI, King, 75–80
Gigs (carriages), 9, 49

Glass Coach, the, 9, 60, 66, 91
Gold State Coach, the, 8, 23, 27, 28, 37, 39, 48, 53, 55, 56, 66, 74–6, 80, 81, 92, 93
Governess Car (carriage), 75, 77
Growlers (carriages), 10

Haflinger ponies, 85, 91
Hammercloth, 9, 48
Hampton Court, 10, 11, 14, 18, 22, 53, 66, 91
Hanover/Hanoverian horses, 21, 27, 28, 51, 52, 53, 54, 66, 73, 91
Hansom Cabs (carriages), 63, 69, 72
Hooper & Co. (coachbuilders), 44, 55, 56, 60, 92
Hutton (coachbuilder of Dublin), 48
Hyde Park, 22, 61, 62, 63

Irish Jaunting Car (carriage), 47
Irish State Coach, 9, 49, 66, 80
Ivory-mounted Phaeton, 43

James I/James VI (of Scotland), 14, 19
James II/James VII (of Scotland), 19

Kensington Palace, 22, 40
Kent, Duchess of, 40
Kent, William, 22
Kew, 39

Lade, Sir John and Lady, 29, 31, 33, 34
Landau (carriage), 9, 25, 39, 42, 43, 53, 55, 67, 72, 80, 83, 91
Louis-Philippe, King of France, 43, 44
Louise, Princess, Duchess of Fife, 62, 63, 69

Margaret, the Princess, 75, 79, 93
Mart, Michael (coachbuilder), 88
Mary I/Tudor, Queen, 8, 11, 14
Mary II, Queen, 19
Maud, Princess/Queen of Norway, 63
May, Princess/Mary, Queen, 63, 67–9, 72–5
Mews, the Royal, 9, 10, 22, 36, 37
Mortlake, Surrey, 14

Napoleon, 27
Nash, John (architect), 36
Nash, Joseph (artist), 44
New Forest ponies, 84

Oldenburg, Count of, 16
Oldenburg, horses, 16
Osborne, Isle of Wight, 45, 49

Peters & Son (coachbuilders), 66
Phaeton (carriage), 8, 9, 28, 33, 34, 35, 36
Philip, HRH The Duke of Edinburgh, 82, 86, 91
Post Chaises (carriages), 33, 41

Ralli-car (carriage), 62
Randem (style of driving three horses), 31
Richmond/Richmond Park, Surrey, 14, 22, 67–9
Rippon, Walter (coachbuilder), 11

Sandringham, 63, 65, 69, 73, 75
Scottish State Coach, the, 9, 91
Sedan Chairs, 15
Selby, Jim, 33
Shetland ponies, 40, 46, 72, 73
Siamese Phaeton (carriage), 45–6
Sleighs/Sledges, 44, 45, 46

Tandem (style of driving two horses), 11, 63, 65, 72
Tattersalls (auction house), 34
Teck, Duke and Duchess of, 67, 68, 69, 91
Telford & Macadam (road engineers), 8, 31, 37

Victoria (carriage), 64
Victoria, Princess, 64
Victoria, Queen, 8, 10, 36, 39–55, 69, 91

Wagonette (carriage), 44, 66, 67, 69
Wales, HRH the Prince Charles, 85–7, 90–1
Wales, Prince of/Edward VII, 55–65
Wales, Prince of/George IV, 28–35
William III, King (of Orange), 19
William IV, King, 8, 37–9, 46
Windsor Castle, 10, 31, 33, 37, 40, 89, 91
Windsor, Duke of (Edward VIII), 71, 73
Windsor greys (horses), 74

York, Albert Duke of (George VI), 69, 73
York, George Duke of (George), 69